JOHNNY DEPP

MOVIE TOP TEN

CREDITS

JOHNNY DEPP: MOVIE TOP TEN
Edited by Jack Hunter
ISBN 1 871592 89 5
© Creation Books & individual contributors 1999
Creation Movie Top Tens: a periodical, review-based publication
First published 1999 by:
Creation Books International
Design/layout/typesetting:
Bradley Davis, PCP International
Cover illustration:
"Donnie Brasco"

Photo credits:
All photos are authorized publicity stills, by courtesy of the BFI, London; Kobal Collection, London; Museum Of Modern Art, New York; and the Jack Hunter Collection.

Copyright acknowledgements:
Every reasonable effort has been made to trace the owners of copyright materials in this book, but in some instances this has proven impossible. The editor and publishers will be glad to receive information leading to more complete acknowledgements in subsequent printings of the book, and in the meantime extend their apologies for any omissions.

British Library Cataloguing in Publication Data:
A catalogue record for this book is available from the British Library

A Butcherbest Production

Creation Books
"Popular books for popular people"

CONTENTS

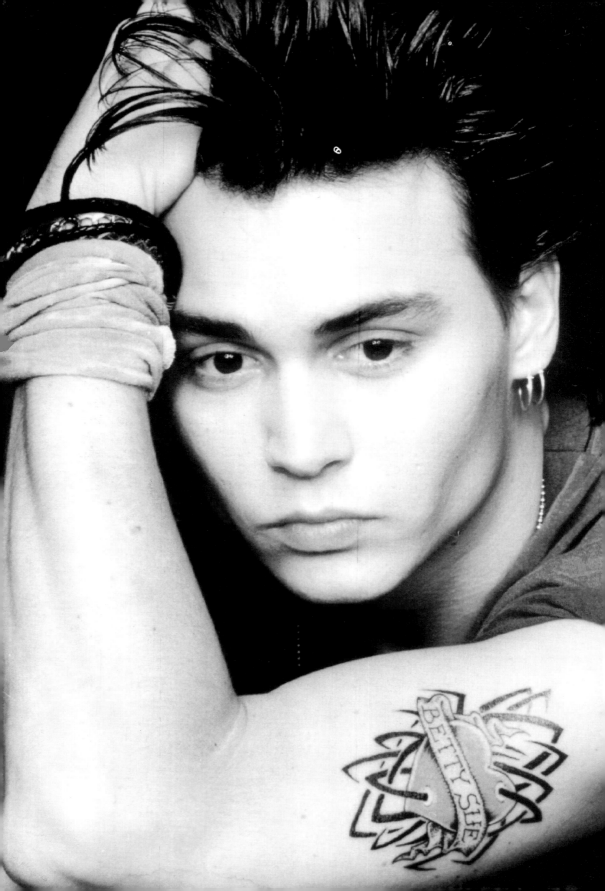

INTRODUCTION:
OUTSIDER EDGE

"Johnny Depp is the best actor of his generation. I think he's capable of anything."

–Terry Gilliam

Consider the standard Hollywood A-List career route: pay dues in straight-to-video or TV, wriggle your way under the nose of a big-name director, hire pushy agent to increase profile and bankability. So far, so Johnny Depp. But from there, it's all in the role choices. While the likes of Bruce Willis, Nicolas Cage and Harrison Ford might squint to see beyond their pay cheques in terms of career validation, Depp seems genuinely unimpressed with the prestige of being the lucrative lynchpin of a blockbuster opening weekend. What's the point of a few more ivory back-scratchers and an ever-swelling battalion of bodyguards if the films stink?

The joy of Johnny Depp is that if he didn't exist, Hollywood would see no need to invent him. He's the most rarefied anomaly: an indie-friendly character actor who rustled himself into the mainstream by taking the road less travelled, waving off commercial, high concept scripts (**Speed, Interview With The Vampire, Legends Of The Fall**) in favour of more personally nourishing projects. As arch and bloody-minded as all of this may seem, Depp has achieved his goal: he's been smart enough to realise that anyone can spend a few weeks in the gym and save the world, and as a result has progressed as an actor and broadened his scope on the casting agents' books. As his **Fear And Loathing In Las Vegas** director Gilliam implies, once you've done a misfit with scissors for fingers, a cross-dressing B-movie film-maker, a lover who thinks he's Don Juan, and a gait-perfect take on America's greatest political philosopher/rogue journalist/chemical-guzzler, is there anything you can't do?

Depp was born in small-town Owensboro, Kentucky, on June 9th, 1963. The family bounced around, living in "probably thirty different houses"[1], before his parents divorced at 15 and he and his mother uprooted to even smaller-town Miramar in southeastern Florida. The boredom was paralysing: "There's Winn-Dixie here, with a drugstore next door, and next to that a card-and-gift store. Across the street was Publix, with its drugstore and card-and-gift store, the same thing only different names. Either way, you were just... there."[2] One afternoon, showing off his fire-breathing skills, Depp accidentally set himself ablaze. His friends put out the fire with their hands, but the scars are still visible on his right cheek.

He dropped out of high school at 16 and headed for Los Angeles with the guitar his mother had bought him when he was 12 ("Puberty was very vague. I literally locked myself in a room and played guitar").[3] His flair for the fretboard impressed a local band, The Flame, and he joined, despite having to be let into clubs by the back door due to being underage. The Flame changed their name to The Kids and enjoyed moderate live success, at one point touring with Iggy Pop. But the Hollywood scene was saturated with strutting young bands, and all of The Kids' members were forced to take day jobs (Depp sold pens over the phone).

At 20, he met make-up artist Lori Allison. The couple soon married and Depp suddenly found himself inside a better connected coterie of LA showbiz life. Allison took him to a party and introduced him to Nicolas Cage. Depp mumbled something about getting into acting and Cage obliged by setting up a meeting with his agent, who put in a call to Wes Craven, then casting for **A Nightmare On Elm Street**. Craven was struggling with the role of Glen, Nancy's luckless boyfriend, and he consulted with his young daughter, who instantly chose Depp. However humble the death-by-mattress experience, **Elm Street**'s busy box-office led to a more high-profile role alongside fellow up-and-comer Rob Morrow in **Private Resort**, an asinine sex-comedy about two predatory adolescents swaggering around a resort hotel. Depp was sufficiently encouraged to take a course of acting lessons at LA's Loft studio and he was soon picked up for an appearance in Oliver Stone's **Platoon**, although most of his screen-time was cut.

Allison and Depp divorced, the movie casting calls soon dried up, and, aside from a few minor TV ventures, Depp suspended his acting career and formed a new band, The Rock City Angels. Then, Fox offered him the part of Detective Tom Hanson in an upcoming TV teen detective drama, *21 Jump Street*, about young-looking cops who go back to high-school, undercover. Each episode ended with a He-Man/Jerry Springer-style to-camera from one of the main characters, summing up the moral issues outlined in the show. Suspecting it to be a step in the wrong direction, Depp refused to even look at the script, worried that committing to the show would render him incapable of taking better jobs or, worse, render him typecast. But his agent managed to present it as a good CV move which, anyway, would probably go the way of 90% of new drama and be cancelled after only one series.

As it happened, *21 Jump Street* made Depp a star. The series was a huge success and, to his continuing embarrassment, Depp was on the cover of every teen-zine in America: "I felt like I was working at a fast-food restaurant. I couldn't stand it. It felt like I was in jail. It had nothing to do with anything that I was about, anything I wanted to do."[4] He got by on forcing himself to see it as an opportunity to fine-tune the skills he'd picked up at The Loft and, after almost four years on the show, he got a call from John Waters.

"I had written **Cry-Baby**," says Waters. "I was trying to think who was going to play this teen idol. So I purposely went and bought all the magazines that I found out later Johnny really hates. He was on the cover of every one of them, and I felt like a paedophile even buying those things! Johnny told me how much he hated being a teen idol, and I said: "Well, stick with us – we'll kill that, we'll get rid of that in a second, because we're going to make fun out of you being a teen idol.'"[5]

Waters cast Depp, alongside Traci Lords and Iggy Pop, as Wade "Cry-Baby" Walker, chief of the "drapes" (delinquents) who falls in love with a middle-class "square" girl in 1954 Baltimore. Aimed more at the nostalgic boomer generation that at Waters' usual camp disciples, **Cry-Baby** is an affectionate parody/celebration of the leather-jacket genre: '50s exploitation movies. A pre-rock-and-roll **Grease** with added prurience. Depp wears the role well, clearly wallowing in the chance to subvert his image and, ideally, confuse his unwanted fanbase.

Editing the dailies during shooting, Waters invited Tim Burton in to take a look. Burton had written a script about a curiously deformed misfit and, having Depp vaguely in mind for the lead, wanted to check the TV star's ability to carry an entire feature. Impressed, he met with Depp and the two immediately realised they shared a similar sense of the absurd. Depp loved the oddball humanity of Burton's screenplay and, finally discovering something he could really pour himself into, confessed to a strong affinity with the role. He moved straight from **Cry-Baby** to work on **Edward Scissorhands**.

"He picks film projects by the script and by directors. That's the best way for him. He's an auteur actor."
–John Waters

Through *21 Jump Street*, Depp had found a twisted kind of fame, but after **Edward Scissorhands**, with co-star Winona Ryder on his arm, he became the new tabloid darling. The couple were engaged and Depp was keen to show off his "Winona Forever" tattoo (later laser-altered to "Wino Forever" after the break-up). Bigger-bucks script offers began to mount, but Depp confounded his agent by refusing them all, determined to take only the jobs that interested him personally. In 1993, he made two fairly low-key films, Emir Kustarica's hugely underrated **Arizona Dream**, in which he got to co-star with Jerry Lewis and fall in love with Faye Dunaway, and **Benny & Joon** (displaced young man models himself on Buster Keaton and falls for a schizophrenic girl). Depp himself had studied the way silent-movie stars like Keaton and Chaplin compensated for the lack of sound by the use of body language and, in both roles, he continued to hone his ability to take a

Benny And Joon

strange, off-centre character and make him real with eye movement and facial expression. It's difficult to see how he could have done that with many of his turn-down parts, particularly the beefy action-himbo lead eventually taken by Keanu Reeves: Jack Traven in **Speed**.

He went even deeper into character with **What's Eating Gilbert Grape?**, a spiky, character-driven film focusing on a young man in a stifling, dead-end town forced to care for his retarded brother and grossly obese, house-bound mother. Gilbert's existence seems to echo Depp's aimless time in Miramar when he was looking after his mother during her depression after his parent's divorce: "It's always taxing to play something that's closer to reality. The two things I inherited from my parents are insanity and chain-smoking."[6]

Later in 1993, he again sought refuge in Burton's bizarre vision, taking the eponymous lead in **Ed Wood**, a brilliantly realised take on the story of Hollywood's leading outsider director. Wood was a cheerful, open transvestite who is widely recognised as being responsible for two of the "worst" films of all-time: **Plan 9 From Outer Space** (title changed from

"Grave Robbers From Outer Space" after church sponsors objected) and **Glen Or Glenda** (the trials of a transvestite played, fittingly, by Wood himself). Wood was a driven man who thought nothing of shoe-horning in garish stock footage to save money, refusing to do re-takes even if his actors had collided with scenery and, most notoriously, replacing his deceased lead in **Plan 9...** (Bela Lugosi) with another actor who cleverly disguised the switch by wearing a cloak over his face. Again, it was a chance for Depp to come in from an angle of emotional, rather than financial, connection to his character.

During the shooting of **Ed Wood**, the tabloid exposure exploded when fellow teen-idol actor River Phoenix collapsed and died from "acute multiple drug intoxication"[7] outside Depp's LA club The Viper Room. It was messy. The American press accused Depp of participating in Phoenix's death by failing to curb back-room drug abuse at the club, while the news networks repeatedly featured a recording of the desperate emergency call placed by Phoenix's brother, Joaquin. Depp closed the club for two weeks, saddened at the way the tragedy was milked as a media event: "The press was trying to tarnish his memory. He was a very sweet guy who made a fatal mistake we're all capable of."[8] In 1994, in a petulant rage, Depp trashed an antique-filled, $1,200-a-night room at New York's Mark Hotel. The bill (reports vary from $2,000 to $10,000) was settled, but a particularly virulent reaction from *The New York Post* was enough to seal his ongoing hatred of hack journalism.

Outside of the less salubrious elements of his public life, Depp's profile was soaring, and he was about to get his chance to work with a few bona fide screen legends. After completing work on Jim Jarmusch's curious stream-of-consciousness western **Dead Man** (also featuring Robert Mitchum and John Hurt), he moved on to Jeremy Leven's **Don Juan DeMarco**, the story of an apparently disturbed man under the impression that he is Don Juan, the world's greatest lover. In **Good Will Hunting** style, "Don Juan" confounds his assigned psychiatrists until he's hooked up with distinguished, seemingly burnt-out Dr Jack Mickler (Marlon Brando). Brando's casting was a condition of Depp's appearance, and, although the two share a certain chemistry, it's undeniable that Brando is coasting. Indeed, director Sidney Lumet once insisted that Brando approaches his jobs by "testing" the director by insisting on two takes of his first key scene; one in which he really puts his soul into the performance, the other in which he delivers only basic textbook technique. If the director prefers the latter, then he simply dumbs down for the rest of the film. True or not, Depp idolised Brando and, in a film where he has to deliver lines like: "Have you ever loved a woman until milk leaked from her? As if she had just given birth to love itself and now must feed it or burst?", he needed all the inspiration he could get.

Don Juan DeMarco

Next up, a turn with Christopher Walken in **War Games** director John Badham's **Nick Of Time**, in which he played a recently bereaved man, kidnapped and, on pain of his daughter's death, forced to murder the State governor within 90 minutes (the running time after the story pre-amble). Walken, a man who once confessed to being persistently stopped on the street, not by people who recognise him as a movie star, but by ex-cons who are convinced they spent time with him in prison, is wonderful – as the bad guy, naturally. Depp is low-key but perfect for the role. The producers clearly wanted someone who could be convincing in an action-oriented film, but who reasoned, rather than blasted his way out of trouble.

After finishing **Nick Of Time**, Depp turned to a more autonomous project: his directorial debut, **The Brave**. This tale of an impoverished native-American father who signs up for a snuff movie to provide for his family was universally deemed a disaster at Cannes '97. Critics accused Depp of elaborate steals from Jarmusch's **Dead Man** and, in casting Brando, simply indulging himself. But, far from adopting the foetal position, he immediately stormed back with easily his most mature performance in a mainstream movie; starring with Al Pacino as FBI mob infiltrator Joe Pistone in Mike

Newell's **Donnie Brasco**.

In the late 1970s, Pistone had all but abandoned his family to go under deep cover with a group of New York wiseguys. He gains the trust of an ageing, low-level foot soldier, Lefty Ruggiero, who, in introducing Joe to his local bosses, endangers his own position ("If I introduce you, I'm responsible for you. Anything wrong with you, I go down.") Joe and Lefty develop a pupil-mentor bond, and, as Joe becomes seduced by the mob lifestyle, his motives and loyalties become blurred. **Donnie Brasco** is an intimate member of the mafia-movie order; it's more about the subtleties of identity and male friendship, a universe away from the lavish insider accounts of Scorsese or Coppola. Again, Depp is the outsider with his nose pressed up against the window of the real world (Edward Scissorhands, Ed Wood). But, in appearing alongside the likes of Pacino, he seemed to be plotting a slightly altered course, eager for recognition as a fully-formed actor. He also seemed keen to mirror Pacino's celebrated preparation method, spending time with the real Joe Pistone; more, he claims, out of respect than artistic validation. "He bought a sensitivity to the part," says Pistone. "That's a side of me that a lot of people don't see. It was amazing. A lot of times during the shoot, I'd close my eyes and say: 'Christ, that's me talking'!"[9]

Back in Christmas, 1995, Depp was in Aspen, Colorado with a group that included then-girlfriend Kate Moss and her mother. They ended up at the Woody Creek Tavern, local hang-out of maverick journalist Hunter S. Thompson, who eventually made his entrance – wielding two sparking cattle-prods. The party headed for Thompson's "fortified compound" home, where, to the dismay of Moss' mother, Thompson invited Depp out back to shoot his beloved nickel-plated shotgun at a propane tank lightly decorated with canisters of nitroglycerine. Depp was hooked. He had read Thompson's masterwork, *Fear And Loathing In Las Vegas*, as a teenager and, as Depp was busy building his acting career, several film-makers were wrestling with the book's difficult cinematic potential (journalist and lawyer travel to Las Vegas for a protracted bout of animalistic, drug-fuelled savagery). In 1980, Bill Murray starred in a loose, forgettable interpretation called **Where The Buffalo Roam**, but then, on Thompson's admission, "drugs became uncool"[10], and efforts were shelved.

In 1996, during shooting of **Donnie Brasco**, Thompson called Depp with the news that Alex Cox was set to attempt a direct interpretation of **Fear In Loathing In Las Vegas** and how did he feel about playing him? A positive reaction from Depp eventually led to a hostile meeting between Cox and Thompson which saw Cox pass the mantle to Terry Gilliam. Depp went to live with Thompson for a while, at one point acting as his agent and bodyguard on a book tour. The plan was similar to that used with Pistone: to absorb Thompson's character so as to play him as truthfully as possible.

"It's not like method acting," claimed Gilliam. "It's more like osmosis."[11]

Thompson and Depp collaborated so closely on transforming Depp into Thompson, that the two would exchange faxes discussing wardrobe test photos. Thompson was suitably blunt, criticising Depp's stance, clothes and hair (eventually, he strapped on a mining light, sat Depp down and styled it himself). Despite his dedication, it's probably Depp's most critically derided film. There is a certain stamina required in enjoying almost two hours of someone else's drug experiences, but **Fear And Loathing In Las Vegas** is far from a disaster. Beyond the hallucinogenic special effects, Gilliam succeeds in presenting the chaos of Thompson's experiences as the ultimate inspiration for his profound asides on the death of the '60s ideal and the hypocrisies of the "American dream", the whole "point" of the book in the first place: a sane man on a trip to the frontline of an insane culture.

A final peek into Depp's future confirms a continuing hunger for the edgier approach. He's just completed London filming on Tim Burton's latest, **Sleepy Hollow**, a typically twisted interpretation of dark fairy-tale "The Legend Of Sleepy Hollow". Soon to open in the States is **The Astronaut's Wife**, in which he stars with Charlize Theron as an astronaut involved in a mysterious accident which forces him to retire from the space program. Along with Terry Gilliam's new film, The Man Who Killed Don Quixote, there are plans to work with Winona Ryder on Michelangelo Antonioni's Just To Be Together, and with Roman Polanski on supernatural thriller The Ninth Gate. There's also talk of a Howard Hughes biopic, and, most intriguingly, a turn as ultra-camp "Mr Showmanship" himself, Liberace.

Whichever way he goes, Depp's reputation as the most accomplished and consistently interesting character actor of his generation is secure. He's the actor's ultimate ideal, picking and choosing his roles entirely on his own terms, with little regard for Hollywood networking and without fear of over-familiarity or marginalisation.

"I think that the movie-going audience would like to see something different, and I think that the Hollywood studio system has underestimated them and fed them pre-fabricated, pre-packaged meat. Not even meat – by-products. I think that's unfortunate and, so, for as long as I'm able to get a job, I would like to be able to say that I did what I wanted."

–Johnny Depp[12]

NOTES

1. *GQ*, October 1993.

2. *GQ*, October 1993.

3. *Cosmopolitan*.

4. *What's Eating Johnny Depp?* Channel 4, 30 December 1998.

5. *What's Eating Johnny Depp?* Channel 4, 30 December 1998.

6. *Vogue*, September 1994.

7. Los Angeles county coroner, Scott Carrier.

8. *Johnny Depp: An Illustrated Story*, David Bassom 1996.

9. *Vanity Fair*, April 1997.

10. *Rolling Stone*, November 1998.

11. *Rolling Stone*, November 1998.

12. *What's Eating Johnny Depp?* Channel 4, 30 December 1998.

TEENAGE WET DREAM: JOHNNY DEPP IN 'A NIGHTMARE ON ELM STREET'

"Johnny Depp has... taken the most risks in his career. He never plays the same part over and over again. He never plays just a matinee idol. He never plays a standard hero. He's always a hero with a flaw, a hero with a weakness, which is incredibly appealing to others. And I think that's the difference:... he takes roles with 'edge'."

—John Waters

Wes Craven's **A Nightmare On Elm Street** (1984), touted as "an innovative horror fantasy that will expose your deepest, primal fear", opens with four teenagers, led by Nancy Thompson (Heather Langenkamp), sharing an identical nightmare about a dead child molester who returns to haunt their dreams. One by one, the teenagers are murdered in the night by Freddy Krueger (Robert Englund), a real-life local child killer who got off on a technicality, was hunted down and burned to death by the town's parents, including Nancy's policeman father (John Saxon). Now, Freddy has returned to torment the children of his old enemies through their nightmares. In the end, Nancy manages to destroy Freddy by drawing him into her reality, and confronting him on her own terms.

Johnny Depp's role in the movie is that of Glen, Nancy's striking, rangy boyfriend – an awkward, endearing character with matted hair, pouty lips and prominent cheekbones. Although not as wild as Tina's delinquent boyfriend Rod (Nick Corri), Glen, in his own way, is something of an outlaw. He lies to his mother about where he's staying, climbs in through Nancy's bedroom window in the middle of the night, and smirks at his parents in a sly, white-trashy kind of way.

Depp's big scene in the movie is that of Glen's nasty, violent death – a scene that is also highly sexualized, in rather an interesting way. Having promised Nancy he'll stay awake until midnight, Glen lounges around on his bed in a white cut-off T-shirt that exposes his tight, tanned midriff. He listens to rock music through his earphones while waiting for "Miss Nude America" to come on TV. Shortly before midnight, he falls asleep, exposing himself to the wrath of a vengeful Freddy who, in a gory and elaborate montage, pulls Glen down through a hole in the center of his bed. A tremendous geyser of blood is then regurgitated through this crater, drenching the walls and ceiling of Glen's bedroom with a vicious splatter of scarlet.

The original script of **A Nightmare On Elm Street** was rejected by all the major studios that director Wes Craven submitted it to, and the process all but bankrupted him. "When I was trying to get funding for **A Nightmare On Elm Street**," says Craven, "I had to earn a living by rewriting other people's scripts. I lost all my savings and I lost my house, which I thought would be my ultimate investment in old age. I'd had to sell that at a loss. It's a long, sad story, ending with me not being able to pay any bills. I had to borrow money... to pay off my taxes"[1].

Once the script found a buyer in New Line Cinema, casting the movie was Craven's most important priority. Heather Langenkamp was cast in the central role of Nancy, having failed to make the final cut of Francis Ford Coppola's **Rumble Fish**. For the part of Nancy's policeman father, Craven chose veteran actor John Saxon, habitué of such low-budget horror films as **Beyond Evil** and **Tenebrae**. For the character of Nancy's tearaway boyfriend Glen, Craven initially wanted a blond, football-player type, a fraternity jock. Instead, the part was given to the skinny, dark-haired, chain-smoking Johnny Depp.

Depp was twenty-one at the time, and newly divorced from singer Lori Ann Allison, with whom he'd been trying to kick-start his rock career. After the divorce, Allison began dating Francis Ford Coppola's nephew, the young Nicolas Cage, who struck up a long lasting friendship with Depp and put him in touch with an acting agent. The first part Johnny auditioned for was Glen in **A Nightmare On Elm Street**. For two nights before the audition, Depp and Cage stayed up all night, running through the lines to make sure Johnny was prepared. Five hours later, his agent called him and told him "you're an actor".

Craven chose Johnny Depp for the part of Glen after listening to the advice of his teenage daughter Jessica, who'd sat in on the auditions. "He has a quiet charisma which none of the other actors had," notes Craven. "Johnny really had that sort of James Dean attraction, a very powerful yet very subtle personality. My teenage daughter and her friends were at the reading and they absolutely flipped over him. He's got real sex appeal for women"[2].

For the scene in which Depp is swallowed whole by his bed and spat out in a stream of blood, Craven decided to use a complicated rotating set. The cameraman and director were strapped into a pair of Datsun car seats, mounted along with the camera rig on one wall of the revolving set. As Depp performed his death throes, the room rotated and one hundred and ten gallons of substitute blood (made from water mixed with starch and colouring agents) was pumped out of the bed, appearing to climb up the walls against the force of gravity[3].

"I love this stuff," Depp told *Fangoria* magazine after shooting the scene. "The kid falls asleep and it's all over. He's sucked right into the bed and spat out as blood. I heard some talk about having a dummy, but I said, 'Hey, I want to do this. It'll be fun. Lemme do it'". An earlier version was shot with a skeleton being ejected from the bed, but this scene didn't make it into the final version of the film.

Although Depp was paid only $1,200 a week for his work on **A Nightmare On Elm Street**, Craven was glad to note that the young actor went on the better things ("I'm gratified by that," says Craven). Depp himself was left totally unfazed by his first movie role. "I got sucked into the bed," he commented, laconically. "What kind of reviews can you get opposite Freddy Krueger? 'Johnny Depp was good as the boy who died'?"[4] And yet the film as a whole garnered a number of very enthusiastic notices. The *New York Times* noted that Wes Craven "specializes in graphically depicted mayhem and gore", and David Edelstein in the *Village Voice* claimed that "Craven's movie drills for fresh nerves", hailing the film as a "minor masterpiece". In Britain, when it was released in September 1985, the *Daily Express* described the film as "a shocker, a hundred per cent nerve tingler", while the *Telegraph* described the film as "admirably crafted". Writing in the *New Statesman*, Francis Wheen found it "most refreshing to see a chiller in which the strongest character by far is female", and *Starburst* saw the film as a significant contribution to the horror genre:

"Craven expertly layers nightmare within nightmare within dreams... delivering the wildest moments to be had in the horror cinema for ages. Craven's visual free rein upturns conventional expectations... it is a film that lingers in the memory."[5]

According to Wes Craven, initial inspiration for the **Elm Street** series came from a number of apparently unrelated articles printed in the *Los Angeles Times* over a period of about a year and a half, during 1980/81. These articles described incidents of people having severe nightmares, and describing them to their families as far worse than any dream they'd ever previously experienced. Claims Craven:

"All of them had a similar reaction – they didn't want to sleep again. They were afraid of going back to the dreams. They tried, one way or another, to stay awake. The next time these people fell asleep, they died. This guy managed to stay awake for three or four days. His family said he was having a nervous breakdown, should take some warm milk and some sleeping tablets – exactly what he didn't want to do. He finally fell asleep and they heard screams and thrashing about. They went to his room and he was dead. An autopsy revealed he hadn't had a heart attack or anything – he was just

dead. They happened so far apart, the newspapers never connected them."[6]

This series of newspaper articles had a profound impact on the director, who testifies to a long-standing fascination with the nature of dreams. When in college, he wrote a research paper on dreaming, and as part of the project was required to keep a journal of his own dream experiences – something which helped with developing the plot of **A Nightmare On Elm Street**. "The dream-world premise had interested me for a long time," says Craven. "In some of my earlier films I'd played with dream sequences where you weren't sure whether the person was dreaming or not. I found that idea intrigued me so much that I wanted to build a film around it."[7] Craven also claims to have based some of the scenes in his various films on his own dream experiences, including **The Hills Have Eyes** (1978), **The Serpent And The Rainbow** (1988) and **The People Under The Stairs** (1992).

Craven also believes that film itself is a dream-like medium in its capacity to distort and expand different forms of consciousness, as in the work of certain European directors. He argues that film is dream-like in its ability to extend and contract time. "It's not like a stage play," he claims. "You can have optical tricks at your beck and call, you can have strange soundtracks, and everything else you can do with film."[8] In fact, **Elm Street** blurs the boundaries between dreaming and waking reality so effectively that it numbs our ability to make any clear-cut distinction between sleeping and waking states – something that makes us question the distinctions we normally make between dream, reality, and representation (ie. film). The movie constantly works on our anxiety about the reliability of that perceptual equipment by which we know "reality". This fusion of film and dream seems particularly significant in relation to the horror genre and its effects, since, as David Edelstein points out in his review of **Elm Street** in the *Village Voice*, "there's an implicit contract between a horror film and its director that dreams don't kill".

Particularly interesting is the fact that Wes Craven should have cast Johnny Depp in a role that is both cute and mischievous, since **A Nightmare On Elm Street** was made long before Depp acquired his off-screen "outlaw" image in the press. Perhaps the director cannily cued in on the young actor's time-worn quality, the hint of grit and fingernail dirt that lurks beneath Johnny's teen-idol looks. And yet, after his role in **Elm Street**, Depp was convinced by his agent to take a role on the TV show *21 Jump Street*, a show which became especially popular with teenage girls. Much to Depp's embarrassment, Fox TV executives began to push him as a teen icon, the ultimate symbol of cool, and the show dragged on for four years. It was only after *21 Jump Street* ended that Depp was able to shed his cute-boy image, which he did by spoofing his teen idol status in John Waters's **Cry-Baby**, where he played a delinquent greaser (Waters claims he imagined Depp as "the best-looking gas station attendant who ever lived[9]).

It didn't take Depp long to be cast in the role of tabloid darling and bad-boy rebel after his involvement in a number of altercations, and after displaying an attitude that garnered him the reputation of something of a nogoodnik. The press quickly began to draw the part-Cherokee actor as an outlaw, a chain-smoking delinquent with yellow fingers and hair that looked like it hadn't been washed any time recently. He also experienced several brushes with the law, including the infamous trashing of his room at the Hotel Mark in New York City, which drove the tabloids into a frenzy. And the death of actor River Phoenix in 1993 of an apparent drug overdose at Depp's rowdy L.A. nightclub, the Viper Room, subjected Depp and his pals to no small amount of unflattering press scrutiny. This reputation for shadiness soon transferred itself to Depp's on-screen image. "Johnny could play a wonderfully sexy mass murderer," says John Waters. "I mean, it's a part made for him. Nobody looks better in rags."[10] "He tells me he has his heart with the outsiders, with the outcast guys," says director Lasse Hallstrom, director of **What's Eating Gilbert Grape?** (1993). "That's the people that he relates the most to."[11]

As many writers and critics of the horror film have pointed out[12], there is an important connection to be made between dreams (especially wet dreams), teenagers (especially rebellious teenagers, like Glen/Johnny Depp), and adolescent sexuality. In this case, the monstrous nature of Glen's death seems closely tied to his rebellious, pubescent sexuality. It's also important to bear in mind the specific invocation of the recurring theme of child abuse in the **Elm Street** series[13] – Freddy, remember, is a child molester who was chased down by a posse of angry parents and burned to death in a furnace in Nancy's basement. Perhaps one of the dramatic strategies of the film is to generate in the adult audience a desire to see the child punished – in this case, punished for his evocation of illicit paedophile desires. It may also be of significance that the children in **A Nightmare On Elm Street** are generally more functional and responsible than the adults (Nancy's mother is an alcoholic, her father is constantly absent from home, Tina's mother neglects her daughter and brings lovers home at night). Certainly, however, it seems clear that the spectacle of what happens to the teenagers' bodies during the course of the film, particularly the violent transformations they undergo during each murder, is the primary appeal of the film to its adult audience.

And if sexual arousal in the audience leads to sexual punishment on the screen, Glen's oral-incorporative bed certainly works as an interesting image of castration[14]. In a rather appropriate way, the glamorously dishevelled Glen/Johnny Depp is punished for his budding sexuality, which, when mixed with his rebelliousness, seems to emphasize the generalized magical powers of children in this film, that in some way seem threatening to adults – both those in the film, and those in its audience. An extra factor in this case, however, is that Glen's teenage body is sucked completely dry of blood, which suggests that perhaps, more than anything else, Glen is the victim of a succubus.

Succubi were mythical demons who descended on their male victims during sleep, and forced them to have sexual intercourse. The victims remained sleeping, but had terrifying nightmares. According to Freudian psychoanalyst Ernest Jones in his book *On The Nightmare*, the succubi attacks handsome youths who are lying half-awake (and who thus submit unresistingly) indulging in sexual antics (Freddy, remember, is a child molester) until their victims get ill and die of exhaustion. It was also believed that the succubi had the capacity to kill their victims by draining them of their blood – as is the case with Glen/Johnny Depp – as well as other vital fluids such as their spinal marrow. The succubi destroyed men by "sucking their strength" during intercourse while they sleep, thereby devouring them, body and soul. Originally, these succubi were the Lilim, or castratory daughters of Lilith, the Devil-snake's consort, and enemy of the sons of Eve in the legend of Genesis.

It is not difficult, according to Jones, to discover the physiological origin of the succubus legend:

"A nightly visit from a ...frightening being, who... withdraws from [the victim] a vital fluid: all this can only point to a natural and common process, namely, to nocturnal emissions accompanied with dreams of a more or less erotic nature. In the unconscious mind blood is commonly an equivalent for semen..."[15]

Thus, in his part as Glen, Johnny Depp is made into a teenage wet dream for the benefit of the adult audience (both male and female), here cast in the role of the predatory succubus. Glen's fatal dream is the audience's reality – the reality of the film – wherein teenage sexuality becomes, to the adults sitting in front of the screen, something magical and seductive, and therefore terribly threatening. Consequently then, as punishment for the desires he arouses, the teenager is summarily put to death – and in a very appropriate way.

NOTES

1. Cit in Brian J. Robb, *Screams And Nightmares: The Films Of Wes Craven*, Titan Books, 1998, p65.

2. Ibid, 68.

3. Ibid., 73.

4. Ibid. 74.

5. All reviews cit in ibid., 77.

6. Ibid., 61–2.

7. Ibid., 62. See also the dream sequences in **Last House On The Left** (1972) and **Deadly Blessing** (1981).

8. Ibid., 63.

9. Cit in Bill Zehme, "Sweet Sensation" (interview with Johnny Depp), *Rolling Stone*, 10th January 1991.

10. Ibid.

11. Cit in *What's Eating Johnny Depp?*, dir/prod. by Adrian Sibley; MBC for Channel 4. Broadcast on Channel 4, Dec 30th 1998, 11.10pm (UK).

12. See, for example, Carol J. Clover, *Men, Women And Chainsaws*, BFI Press: London, 1992; James Iaccino, *Psychological Reflections On Cinematic Terror: Jungian Archetypes In Horror Films*, Greenwood Press, Westport, CT., 1994; James Twitchell, *Dreadful Pleasures: An Anatomy Of Modern Horror*, OUP, Oxford, 1987.

13. Like most high-grossing slasher movies, **A Nightmare On Elm Street** is now no longer a film, but a series. Working on the principle that there is pleasure in re-asserting the same terror, Freddy Krueger vitally resurges in the dreams of countless teenagers in a number of sequels to the original movie. Johnny Depp, grateful to this day to Wes Craven for giving him his first big break, graciously appeared in the (supposedly) last **Elm Street** sequel (**Freddy's Dead: The Final Nightmare**, 1991) as a cameo murder victim. The popularity of this and the subsequent sequels suggests that audiences of this kind of horror film have a need to stay with the narrative, perhaps to confirm their suspicions that the bastion of the family cannot be so easily defended (for a further discussion of this point, see William Paul, *Laughing Screaming – Modern Hollywood Horror And Comedy*, Columbia University Press, New York 1994:414). In each of these sequels, as is the convention in the horror film, the villain returns as an increasingly sardonic figure of terror who constantly avoids ultimate defeat – a necessarily formulaic convention. Moreover, according to Ernest Jones, the horror film is repetitive "precisely because death and malformation have to be presented in rigid conventions, or disgust would overwhelm curiosity". In other words, it is repetitive because it is a depiction, both fantastic and highly conventionalized, "of what happens to flesh, of the fate of being a

body" (see Ernest Jones, *On The Nightmare*, Liveright Publishing Corporation, NY: 125).

14. In fact, the destructive/castratory bed is a more common image in film and literature than one might suspect; see, for example, Wilkie Collins' "A Traveller's Tale Of A Terribly Strange Bed" and the filmic variants of this suffocating four-poster, including William Castle's fascinating **13 Ghosts** (1960).

15. Jones, 120–122.

'PLATOON'

Even the most sweet-talking, placatory agent would find it difficult to make the case that Johnny Depp's role in Oliver Stone's 1986 film **Platoon** is large. In truth, the actor is barely on screen for five minutes in total and only has two speaking scenes. However, Depp's achievement in landing a part in such a heavyweight film at such an early stage in his journey through celluloid, the type of role he plays, and his experiences of the shoot and subsequent critical appraisal of the film all have a significant impact on his future career. **Platoon** was his first "serious" picture and one that bears examination regardless of the size of his role in it.

Platoon immediately flashes its heavyweight credentials by opening on a black screen with a Biblical quotation written in white: "'Rejoice O young man in thy youth...' –Ecclesiastes". The gesture is typical of Oliver Stone, surely one of the most portentous directors ever to shout "action". He immediately asserts his film as an important work with something very definite to say that ought to be paid very close attention. You get the feeling that questions may be asked as you leave the cinema.

The opening scene sees new recruits, the young men of Ecclesiastes, disembark from the hatch of a transport plane into the heat and dust of Vietnam. This callow company of men includes Chris Taylor (Charlie Sheen). As soon as they leave the plane, black body bags are loaded in, an immediate reminder of human frailty, mortality and the probable fate that awaits the fresh-faced troops. Stone's film assumes the proportions of classical tragedy, where the inevitability of death hangs over the stage as soon as the curtain is raised. The recruits walk past a ragged, bedraggled platoon returning from their tour of duty. "You're gonna love the Nam!" yell these jaded grunts with the blackest of irony, and there is a poignant moment as Taylor catches the haunted eyes of one of them. It is, perhaps, a vision of his own future. The tagline of **Platoon** is "The first casualty of war is innocence" and in this masterly opening scene innocence and experience collide as wonderfully as in any William Blake poem. The first stirrings of Samuel Barber's "Adagio For Strings" only adds to the elegiac feel.

From here Stone takes us in a helicopter looking down on the verdant treetops. A title makes it specific: "September 1967 – Bravo Company, 25th Infantry somewhere near the Cambodian border". Next we're inside the sepulchral darkness of the jungle. Taylor, exhausted by the humidity as it is, chances upon some corpses (more reminders of mortality) and vomits. Sergeant Barnes (Tom Berenger) shouts at him, but Sergeant Elias (Willem Dafoe) helps lighten his pack. Taylor collapses.

The company sets camp, while Taylor writes a letter to his grandmother in voiceover. He doesn't think he'll be able to make it through his allotted year in Vietnam. The camera cuts through the camp, resting briefly on many of the troops. Lerner (Johnny Depp) makes his first appearance, apparently sharing a joke with Elias. Elsewhere, the platoon officers discuss tactics. They decide that the new recruits should go on look-out duty.

On duty Taylor, in voiceover again, delivers the first great dialogue of the film: "Maybe I've finally found it, way down here in the mud. Maybe from down here I can start up again, be something I can be proud of without having to fake it, be a fake human being." Junior (Reggie Johnson) falls asleep during his watch. Taylor awakes to find the Viet Cong approaching. In the ensuing fire fight, one man dies and Taylor is wounded. Junior claims Taylor fell asleep at his post. Barnes yells at Taylor.

Back from hospital, Taylor and King empty the camp latrines. When night falls, King (Keith David) takes Taylor to a dug out where, to the sounds of Jefferson Airplane's "White Rabbit" and Smokey Robinson's "Tracks Of My Tears" he smokes marijuana for the first time with other like-minded men from the camp. This is another, happier loss of innocence for Taylor. Elias blows smoke from a joint into Taylor's mouth through the barrel of a rifle. Depp, as Lerner, is in this scene, playing guitar while wearing a white vest and headband. He resembles some outrageously good-looking rock star who took a wrong turn at Woodstock and ended up in Hanoi. As a former lead guitarist in the moderately successful Florida band The Kids, who opened shows for big names like Talking Heads and Iggy Pop in the early '80s, Johnny Depp must have felt right at home in this scene.

A scene from the barracks is in direct contrast to the jovial freakdom preceding. They listen to country and western, play cards and talk about women. The mood is hostile. Lieutenant Wolfe (Mark Moses) visits and it is obvious his men do not respect him.

"New Year's Day, 1968. Just another day, staying alive" announces Taylor in voiceover as the platoon make their way through the jungle. They find an abandoned bunker complex, but it is booby-trapped and one soldier has his arms blown off. They then discover another American soldier killed and tied to a tree.

Enraged and intent on revenge, the platoon descend on a Vietnamese village and search it for Viet Cong. In a thatched hut, Taylor finds a hiding place and forces two civilians – an old woman and her son – to leave it. Exhaustion and fear turn to rage as he screams at the son and shoots at the ground in front of him. Coming to his senses, he is plainly shocked by the cruelty of his actions. Bunny (Kevin Dillon) clubs the son to the ground with his rifle and repeatedly hits him with it until his skull splits open. Taylor weeps.

Elsewhere, Barnes interrogates the head man of the village. Lerner, a translator, puts Barnes's questions to the head man in Vietnamese. Lerner tells Barnes that the head man claims the North Vietnamese Army have not been in the village for months. He seems to be pleading for clemency on behalf of the old man when he suggests that it might have been a lone Viet Cong scout who killed the soldier tied to a tree. However, Barnes shouts Lerner down. The head man's wife enters the scene and starts shouting at Barnes. Lerner translates. Barnes shoots the old woman in the head. Lerner looks shocked. At this point, the word "Sherilyn" is plainly visible on the side of Lerner's helmet. This refers to Sherilyn Fenn, the seventeen-year-old actress who Depp had started seeing shortly before he was cast in **Platoon**. They dated for two years, but it would be 1990 before she found real fame as Audrey Horne, the schoolgirl who could tie knots in cherry stalks with her tongue, in David Lynch's surrealist TV series *Twin Peaks*.

After the shooting, many of the platoon look sick and uneasy, but others are given new bloodlust. Barnes is relentless. He orders a reluctant Lerner to tell the head man that other villagers will die unless he informs on the Viet Cong. Lerner hesitates then complies. Barnes threatens to kill the head man's daughter. Elias turns up and he and Barnes fight. Lieutenant Wolfe separates them and orders the platoon to burn the village. As the huts go up in smoke, Taylor prevents the rape of a child. Lerner is seen carrying another child to safety from the burning village.

Back at camp, Elias threatens Barnes with a court martial for his illegal killing. The platoon divides in two as the men take sides. "I can't believe we're fighting each other when we should be fighting them" is how Taylor puts it. At night, Elias and Taylor watch the stars together, Elias confesses he no longer believes in what he is doing.

On another mission the platoon are ambushed and Lerner, who is ahead of the rest of the troops, is shot. Taylor goes ahead and brings him back behind friendly lines. Clearly in a lot of pain, Lerner pleads with Taylor not to be left alone. Taylor reassures him, but must go. This is Johnny Depp's last appearance in **Platoon**.

More fighting ensues and Elias strikes out on his own. Barnes goes after him and kills him. Taylor encounters Barnes shortly afterwards and the sergeant tells the grunt that Elias was killed by Viet Cong. However, as the platoon leave in helicopters they see Elias fleeing the jungle pursued by Viet Cong. In one of cinema's most enduring images, he falls to his knees, raises his arms in a pose that recalls the crucifixion and slumps forward dead. Taylor realises that Barnes has killed Elias. Back in the stoner's dug-out, Taylor tries to persuade his friends in the platoon to kill Barnes. The sergeant appears and he and Taylor fight. Taylor is beaten.

The platoon returns to the scene of the recent fighting. King receives orders to return home. Night falls and the platoon sit in their foxholes. The N.V.A attacks. It is a massacre. Barnes and Taylor confront each other on the battlefield. Barnes is about to kill him when he is prevented by the fall of bombs.

Taylor wakes on the battlefield at dawn. He is surrounded by corpses. He finds Barnes, who is injured. Taylor kills Barnes.

New soldiers appear and Taylor leaves the scene by helicopter. His closing monologue in voiceover is surely the real sentiments of Oliver Stone, himself a veteran of Vietnam, when it came to writing and making this wonderful film: "The war is over for me now, but it will always be there, the rest of my days... those of us who did make it have an obligation to teach to others what we know, and to try with what's left of our lives to find a goodness and meaning to this life."

When Johnny Depp signed up for **Platoon** he had already played significant parts in Wes Craven's 1984 schlock horror **A Nightmare On Elm Street**, George Bowers's 1985 sex comedy **Private Resort** (a film he prefers to leave off his official resumé these days), and the 1986 made-for-TV thriller **Slow Burn**. At this point he was beginning to consider himself an actor rather than a musician who stepped in front of the camera to play the bills. "It wasn't like I ever kissed the guitar goodbye," he told US magazine. "But I seemed to be having more steam with acting." However, job offers were almost non-existent and Depp was considering giving up on the movie business when Oliver Stone asked him to read for the part of Lerner, the young translator in **Platoon**.

The audition was apparently a fraught experience, the 23-year-old actor terrified by the driven director. Nonetheless, he got the gig and soon found himself in the Philippines for a ten-week shoot which would make being eaten by a bed in **Elm Street** seem like a pat on the back.

Stone wanted his actors to experience something approaching the hardships of war so that they could give truthful performances. This meant a gruelling training programme devised by Dave Dye, a Vietnam vet brought on board as a consultant. Depp had to dig fox holes in full military uniform, eat basic food from a ration tin, get used to the heat, insects and dirt and learn how to handle a machine gun. When training finished, Depp spent 54 days getting up at 5AM and acting in the humid jungle of the Philippines. This was tough, but was also just the kind of fiery baptism which would prepare him for the **Edward Scissorhands** shoot four years later. Although Tim Burton's movie was shot in the relative comfort of Florida, the heavy make-up and clothes, and cumbersome prosthetic hands made filming a physical challenge for Depp.

But Stone's insistence that his cast and crew give their all paid off. **Platoon** opened on 19 December 1986, initially in only six cinemas, but ended up taking $136 million at the US box office and winning four Oscars for Best Picture, Best Director, Best Screenplay and Best Cinematography. The *Los Angeles Times* sounded a note matched by many critics by writing that "War movies of the past, even the greatest ones, seem like crane shots in comparison. **Platoon** is at ground zero."

The film, which had cost only $6.5 million to make, was a major critical and commercial success. The actor and director Vincent Gallo would later remark of Johnny Depp that he has been able to permeate the mainstream without pandering to it. That may be a trick he learned from **Platoon**, a film with mass appeal which never compromises or pulls any punches. Johnny Depp's first serious film role, like the actor himself, is a masterclass of artistic integrity.

But the success of **Platoon** was bittersweet for Johnny Depp. When he finally saw the finished film he was dismayed to discover that most of his performance and almost all of his dialogue had been left on the cutting room floor. To be fair, a good fifteen per cent of the script was chopped in editing, but it does seem strange that so much of one actor's work should be lost. Details are sketchy as to why this should be so, but Depp has suggested that it was because he changed and ad libbed so much of his dialogue. This is something the actor, always keen to take as active a role as possible in the creative development of his projects, continues to do to this day. However, attempting to change the carefully considered words of such a tempestuous and experienced a figure as Oliver Stone on the hoof shows that Depp has never lacked either confidence or cheek. He can't have annoyed Stone too much, though – the director tried to cast him again in 1990 when he was putting together **The Doors**, but it never quite came together.

Oliver Stone has also indicated that he cut so much of Depp out because he was too similar to Charlie Sheen's character. Because we see so little of Lerner, we can only speculate where those similarities lie. Certainly, they are both positive figures in Oliver Stone's moral universe. When we first see Lerner, he is sharing a joke with Elias, the "good angel" of the two sergeants who exert an influence of Taylor's development. We next encounter Lerner in the dug out, smoking pot with Elias and others. Lerner then has his biggest scene, interpreting and pleading with Barnes on behalf of the Vietnamese head man. He later carries a child to safety from the burning village. Finally, he himself is carried to safety by Taylor.

Taylor is an innocent abroad in the fallen world of Vietnam. If the full Lerner part was written in a similar way, then that would make **Platoon** the first of many films in which Johnny Depp plays just this kind of character. A gentle monster in fast-buck America (**Edward Scissorhands**), a stranger who looks like he just stepped out of a silent movie finding a home and relationship in the contemporary world (**Benny And Joon**), a deluded idealist in a jaded Hollywood (**Ed Wood**), a beatific accountant in the grotesque and violent Wild West (**Dead Man**) – all these roles and arguably many of his others see Johnny Depp cast as an almost childlike naïf immersed in a corrupt environment. **Platoon** could be regarded as the film that gave him a taste for the oddball, outsider parts which have become his stock-in-trade.

Platoon is also typical of his later work in that Depp gives an ostensibly masculine character a feminine spin. With his androgynous looks, Johnny Depp recalls those Hollywood male leads who were beautiful rather than hunky, stars like Montgomery Clift and James Dean. Appropriately, he has built a career on playing weepy gang members, sensitive cowboys and transvestite movie directors who parachute into combat wearing women's underwear. Lerner is a grunt in Vietnam, surely one of the most manly jobs you can have, but we never see him in combat. We see him playing guitar, maternally carrying a child and speaking to Barnes on behalf of an old Vietnamese woman. This maternalism will later manifest itself in **Ed Wood**, where Johnny Depp's character replaces Bela Lugosi's estranged wife in caring for the veteran actor, and in **What's Eating Gilbert Grape?** where, as the long-haired title character, Depp must look after his family on behalf of a mother too obese to even leave the house.

Fathers rather than mothers are important to Oliver Stone in **Platoon**. Referring to Barnes and Elias, Taylor refers to himself as a "child born of those two fathers". This idea of an adopted father-figure will manifest itself again and again in Depp's films. Vincent Price in **Edward Scissorhands**, Iggy Pop in **Cry-Baby**, the Indian Nobody in **Dead Man**, Al Pacino in **Donnie Brasco** – all play paternal roles. In real life, too, Depp seems to gravitate towards older male mentors like John Waters, Tim Burton, Marlon Brando and Hunter S. Thompson.

The scene in **Platoon** where Lerner acts as translator is a key moment for understanding the rest of Depp's career. When Lerner translates the hysterical babblings of the old Vietnamese woman for Barnes, he places himself at a meeting point between gender, culture, race and language. He literally speaks the old woman's lines and seems to take her side, but he also interprets Barnes's threats to her in aggressive Vietnamese. This sense of fitting in nowhere is, as discussed above, highly appropriate in terms of Depp's future roles. However, it is also indicative of the actor's later standing in the film industry. The translator who slips easily between cultures is the actor who is welcome in glitzy Hollywood, but prefers not to embrace it fully, who can command millions of dollars for a film appearance, but who has appeared in few commercially successful films, who was born in Kentucky but moved to Florida and now calls the world his home.

But this level of success might always have eluded Johnny Depp had he not felt so disillusioned by his experiences on **Platoon**. Having worked his guts out in unpleasant conditions only to find most of his performance cut, Depp decided that his next project would be a big-paying piece of television fluff filmed in Vancouver. When he was first offered the lead (a fresh-faced detective who goes undercover in a high school) in *21 Jump Street* he turned it down on the grounds that such work was beneath a veteran of an Oscar-winning movie. But, thanks to Stone's liberal use of the editing scissors, he was feeling unsure of his own talents. What's more, he was broke and living in Nicolas Cage's one-room Los Angeles apartment, living on loose change that he found in drawers – he couldn't resist the lure of television for long. *21 Jump Street* ran for three years between 1987–1990, paid $45,000 per episode and made Depp a major star. It allowed him to get any film role he wanted, but his formative work on **Platoon**, where he was Lerner by name and learner by nature, would define the sort of roles he chose and the approach he would take to them. Depp may have lost the battle in **Platoon**, but it helped him go on to win the Hollywood war.

TEEN ICON: NOTES ON JOHN WATERS' 'CRY-BABY'

"If I can have a hit in mid-America... that would be the most devious thing I could do"

—John Waters

John Waters' **Cry-Baby** is, in many ways, an uncomfortable film in the director's cannon. Famous for producing films that glorified in good-bad taste, and earned him the nickname the Pope of Trash from cult author William Burroughs, Waters' films demarcated a terrain of excessive campy chaotic mayhem defined by a celebration of the outsider as against the all-American family. Utilizing a regular cast – called the Dreamlanders – made up predominately from childhood friends, assorted misfits, pre-punk punks, and anti-hippies, Waters' most famous/notorious low-budget, thoroughly independent movies were produced in the seventies: **Multiple Maniacs** (1970), **Pink Flamingos** (1972), **Female Trouble** (1974) and **Desperate Living** (1977). Shot in and around his native Baltimore, these films glorified in images of anarchic obscenity, and a humour that was gleefully, outrageously, gross (an aesthetic which is most clearly exemplified in the legendary climatic scene of **Pink Flamingos** in which Divine, a three hundred pound transvestite[1], anxious to prove his/her prowess as the filthiest person alive, scoops a recently excreted canine turd into his/her hand and – putting it to his/her mouth – proceeds to gobble it down). These justifiably legendary films were screened as midnight movies throughout the seventies and early eighties, and earned Waters – and his star Divine – a loyal cult following[2].

As the seventies came to an end, so Waters' aesthetic developed and changed, the rage and desire to confront people began to be tempered; partly this was due to Waters' desire to progress as a filmmaker – to repeatedly make **Pink Flamingos** style-gross outs for cult audiences would be a redundant gesture, and the progression emphasized a desire to reach larger audiences.

The Dreamlanders grew up making movies and causing mayhem together, but over the years various members of the close knit group died (David Lochary, Edith Massey) or drifted into other careers or aspects of film production (such as Pat Moran, who has concentrated on working as a Waters' casting director and production assistant). In 1981 Waters directed **Polyester**, his first film to be financed by New Line Cinema, and his largest budget thus far ($300,000), which enabled him to cast Tab Hunter in a small role. This would set the trend for Waters' future casting, which would combine a mixture of Dreamlanders, cult actors, bizarre personalities and celebrities.

Following **Polyester** Waters – again financed by New Line Cinema – directed his first 'acceptable' movie: **Hairspray** (1988). Set around the fictional Corney Collins Show, an early evening teenage dancing and music programme, and based on an actual Baltimore TV show called The Buddy Deane Show, **Hairspray** saw the introduction of a clear social message (of sorts) into a Waters' film for the first time, with its theme of inter-racial romance and the collapse of segregation in Baltimore. Although infinitely more palatable than his earlier works, **Hairspray** nevertheless still featured Waters' regular leading woman Divine, with Dreamland regular Mink Stole, alongside the newly discovered Ricki Lake, and celebrity cameos by Blondie's Debbie Harry, singer Sonny Bono, starlet Pia Zadora, and The Cars' Ric Ocasek. Tragically Divine, who had appeared in all but one of Waters' features – or "Divine/John Waters vehicles"[3] as Waters would describe these films – died a mere two weeks after the opening of the movie.

Waters' next movie **Cry-Baby** was the first movie to be directed by Waters following the loss of Divine. The film was also Waters' first Hollywood feature, with a budget of ten million dollars coming from Imagine Entertainment, and the finished film being distributed by Universal. To some extent it could never succeed – not only did the film lack the on-screen presence of Divine, who attracted a large section of the audience, but some hardcore Waters fans inevitably believed that the film was a "sell-out"[4]. As Jack Stevenson has observed: "Its story failed to win over new audiences or interest the old fans while its period stylizations were considered by some as too slick...(...)... he was making movies *about* teenage angst whereas before he had made movies *out of* teenage angst"[5].

Cry-Baby is set in 1954, focusing on the graduating class of a Baltimore High School which is divided between the ultra straight suburban upper-middle class Squares and the hep street smart white trash Drapes. The Squares are led by ultra-clean cut Baldwin (Stephen Mailer), who dreams of normality, whilst the Drapes – "common juvenile delinquents" – are led by leather jacket clad Wade "Cry-Baby" Walker (Johnny Depp). Baldwin is dating Allison (Amy Locane), but Allison is "tired of being good" and is attracted to the J.D: Cry-Baby.

At the conservative Square RSVP talent contest Baldwin and his friends perform a doo-wop number, whilst Allison performs a romantic love song. Cry-Baby arrives at the contest and invites Allison to watch him sing with his band-cum-gang The Cry-Baby Combo at Turkey Point ("the redneck Riviera"), a ramshackle shack-cum-bar decorated with cross-and-stars flags, where Cry-Baby lives in a shack that is equal parts Addams Family and Clampetts, with his grandmother Ramona Rickettes (Susan Tyrell) and Uncle Belvedere

(Iggy Pop), who have made him – he states – "The happiest juvenile delinquent in Baltimore". To the chagrin of Baldwin, Allison's grandmother – Mrs Vernon-Williams (Polly Bergen) – allows Allison to attend the performance by Cry-Baby. At Turkey Point Allison meets Cry-Baby's single-mom-and-pregnant-again sister Pepper (Ricki Lake) – "she's pregnant, but she can fight like a man!" growls Cry-Baby – and his friends/gang members: Hatchet Face (Kim McGuire), Wanda (Traci Lords) and Milton (Darren Burrows). At the performance Cry-Baby invites Allison to join him on stage and the two sing together, while local slut Lenora (Kim Webb) who is watching in the audience radiates jealousy.

Following the show the gang retreat into couples and begin to make-out. Cry-Baby tells Allison that he is an orphan, his father was the notorious Alphabet Bomber: "Bombs exploding in the airport, barbershop..." Allison states, to which Cry-Baby replies: "that's right, all in alphabetical order, car-wash, drug store...". His father was given the electric chair; worse, Cry-Baby states: "my mum couldn't spell – but they fried her too!" To honour the memory of his executed parents Cry-Baby is compelled to perform one criminal act everyday, and sheds a single tear for this transgression. Allison tells Cry-Baby that she too is an orphan, her parents died in two freak airplane accidents. Before the couple can talk more the Squares attack the Drapes, setting fire to Cry-Baby's motorbike. The police arrive and arrest all

of the Drapes.

At court the Drapes are fined, Pepper's children are sent for adoption, and Cry-Baby is sent to jail until he's twenty-one. Cry-Baby confesses his love to Allison as he is led away. Outside the jail the ever-jealous Lenora has arranged for the press to photograph her with the handcuffed Cry-Baby, claiming she is pregnant with his child.

The following day Allison – believing the newspaper reports that Cry-Baby is the father of Lenora's child, agrees to sing with Baldwin and the Squares at the opening of the Enchanted Forest theme park. In jail Cry-Baby is scheduled to have a whiffle-cut and lose his long hair, he has a single tear tattooed on his face, he tries to escape the jail by crawling through the drains, but ends up in the barbershop. Meanwhile, Pepper, Ramona and Belvedere disguise themselves as Squares and go to the orphanage to adopt Pepper's children. Here all the children are on display in small glass-fronted rooms, akin to the reptile house of a zoo, each child performing a mundane household chore in the hope that he or she will be adopted as useful. Pepper's children – Snare Drum and Suzy Q – have been dressed as conjoined twins to dissuade any potential adoption, but they – and all the other children

– are freed by the family.

At the opening of the amusement park Belvedere rescues Allison from the stage, where she is being humiliated by the Squares who will not let her sing as she wants. Mrs Vernon-Williams, recognising Cry-Baby as honourable, backs the Drapes. The entire gang drive to the jail and demand Cry-Baby's release.

Cry-Baby is released by popular demand, but at the release Baldwin taunts Cry-Baby, telling the masses that it was his grandfather that executed Cry-Baby's father. Cry-Baby challenges Baldwin to a chicken run with a difference – each of them will be hanging onto the roof of their respective gangs cars. Cry-Baby wins the chicken run whilst Pepper gives birth in the back of the car. Allison races to greet him on the back of a motorbike, the motorbike skids and she is catapulted in her underwear through the air before landing in Cry-Baby's open arms. The entire Drape gang shed single tears.

Whilst Water's previous film, **Hairspray**, had utilized nostalgia, and located itself within the milieu of early sixties Baltimore, it retained a sense of timelessness, with its self-knowing references to metacultural events (for example Divine's character Edna Turnblad unwittingly quoting Bob Dylan, or with Pia Zadora's hilarious appearance as an archetypal beatnik reading from Alan Ginsberg's *Howl*). Cry Baby, however, utilized an almost classic love-against-all-odds narrative, and appears on initial viewing to be closer to kitsch quasi-fifties pseudo-nostalgia-crap such as **Grease** (Randal Kleiser, 1978) or **American Graffiti** (George Lucas, 1973) than the classic Waters' oeuvre.

However, whilst **Cry-Baby** may superficially appear to bear the hallmarks of these seventies nostalgia films, it also pertains to the more classic John Waters' interests of crime (the film was loosely inspired by the actual murder of a Drape in Baltimore which became a moral reference point for the nuns at Waters' school), exploitation movies and trash culture, and specifically the fifties juvenile delinquency pictures (a genre that is defined via the themes of outcast greasers, petty crime, switchblades, chicken runs, and rebellion) to which the film pays homage. Further, the film emphasizes the gang/extended family above the nuclear family, a recurring theme in all of John Waters' films, from Divine's gang of outcasts and freaks in **Pink Flamingos** through to the crazed Lesbian runaways in **Desperate Living**. Like his previous work **Cry-Baby** celebrates rock and roll, already identified by Waters as a sneering contempt for the normal and a celebration of the outsider/s (see, for example the imaginative usage of the classic "Surfing Bird", used to accompany a garishly puckering, "singing" asshole in the transgressive **Pink Flamingos**, or the entire soundtrack of Waters' **Mondo Trasho** [1969]). The film also

contains several classic John Waters' motifs and scenes, for example; cool criminals (the Alphabet Bomber), the surrealistic orphanage, the absurd presentation of sex (in **Cry-Baby** this is best articulated by the French-kissing scene, which parodies the fixation on kissing and making-out amongst teenagers in mainstream movies), the lurking pornographer desperate to get the Drape girls to model for him, and the celebration of the offensive (in the case of **Cry-Baby** this is manifested in the gleefully happy and endlessly pregnant teen-mom Pepper, who dreams of having triplets). Most importantly, however, the film is cast with the outré personalities that have always fascinated Waters and which – by the time the film was in production – were becoming another Waters' trademark; as he would later state: "the cameo casting in **Cry-Baby** was a gimmick"[6].

Amongst the support cast of **Cry-Baby** are numerous cult figures, including Traci Lords in one of her first non-sex roles (Lords was the star of dozens of hardcore sex films, and the source of a minor scandal when it was discovered she had begun her porno career at the age of sixteen). Waters' describes Traci Lords in **Cry-Baby** as looking "like Patty McCormack [from the film **The Bad Seed** [Mervyn LeRoy, 1956] grown up"[7]. Also appearing in the movie are one-time teen idol Troy Donahue (star of the TV series *Surfside Six*

[1960-62] and *Hawaiian Eye* [1962-63]), punk-rock legend Iggy Pop, and Warhol/Morrissey actor Joe Dallasandro (star of **Lonesome Cowboys** [1968], **Trash** [1970], and **Heat** [1972], amongst others) who appears as the evangelist Bible-bashing father of Milton, one of Cry-Baby's gang members. However the film's most bizarre cameo is an appearance by Patricia Hearst, the one time hostage of the seventies' revolutionary group the S.L.A, as Wanda's hopelessly naive mother.

With the absence of the irreplaceable Divine, a reference point for many of Waters' audience, Waters had to find a new lead, and decided to make **Cry-Baby** his first "boy" film, in other words his first film with a "classic" male lead. Waters researched youth stars by purchasing dozens of teenage magazines and by talking to Pat Moran's teenage daughter. Depp – then appearing in the TV series *21 Jump Street* – was ubiquitous, appearing in almost all of the teen-mags Waters' brought. Waters knew he had found his leading man; besides, as he would later comment, "the only other person who could have played it was Charles Starkweather, and he was dead"[8]. Waters' gesture was a brave one – as Depp would later write – Waters had "really stuck his neck out"[9] in casting him.

Johnny Depp was suited to the part of Wade "Cry-Baby" Walker; not only was Depp a bona fide teen idol, but he also was able to recognize the absurdity of being labelled as such: "John Waters had read some stories on me in teen magazines, and he picked up on this reluctance I had to be... labelled and pinned down. He still teases me about the fact that the way he found out about me is the very thing that I hate, which is teen garbled weirdness. One of the reasons I did the movie is that it really made fun of being labelled"[10]. The film enabled Depp to step out of the clichéd teen idol role by playing with this persona and transforming it via an exaggerated pastiche. Thus, in **Cry-Baby**, Depp is able to blow up (literally and metaphorically) the classic gestures of the cinematic-teen-star, and he turns in a performance that echoes every youth icon the fifties – part Elvis Presley sneer, and part James Dean sensitive – yet it is clear that the figure being lampooned most throughout the performance is that of Johnny Depp-as-star. Undoubtedly this deconstruction of Depp's perceived public teen star persona was a collaborative effort with Waters, who shot such scenes as Depp crawling through the prison's sewers – hardly the traditional image of a teenage icon. As Depp would recall: "John had taken a chance on me to spoof my 'given' image in **Cry-Baby**"[11].

By casting Depp in the role of Cry-Baby, Waters was able to subvert the public perception of Depp as star, and the film takes a clear pleasure in challenging the absurd sanctity of youth icons (not least by placing Depp in a gang with a famous ex-porn starlet). The film allowed Depp to reveal a degree of self-awareness about the construction of his media persona, moreover the film enabled Depp to reach an audience beyond the given teenage demographic of much of his previous work. Further, Waters' benefited from having a Hollywood star in his movie, with the film playing in fifteen hundred American theatres, a measure of success given that **Hairspray** had only played in a little more than two hundred. "The only way I could do terrorism at my age – at this position in my career – would be to do a Hollywood movie that could reach every person and make them crazy"[12].

      Cry-Baby represents Waters' at a point of transformation in his career between independent filmmaker and Hollywood filmmaker. It also represents Depp's initial move against what he perceived as his destiny, which, as he saw it, lay "somewhere between *Chips* and *Joanie Loves Chaachi*"[13], a move he would fully consolidate in his work with the director Tim Burton. Waters – who had stated "My ultimate goal is to work my most pernicious ideas into the most mainstream product"[14] – was able to increase his audience, and establish himself as a potential Hollywood filmmaker, and indeed he would go on to make his best mainstream film three years later, with the acclaimed and subversive **Serial Mom** (1993). Nevertheless, **Cry-Baby** offers an intriguing juncture in two important careers.

NOTES

1. The term "transvestite" does little justice to the persona and appearance of Divine, whose appearance mocked traditional cross-dressers. Divine's look – especially in the seventies – was thanks in part to the vision of long-time Waters associate, and ugly expert, Van Smith who devised the monstrous/humorous Divine look. Prior to the arrest of Charles Manson, Divine used to state in his Waters-scripted terrorist drag performances that he had killed Sharon Tate.

2. Now all but relegated to the darker recesses of history thanks in part to video technologies and the growth of the multiplex culture, midnight movies were the definitive space in which to view sex, trash, genre, and exploitation cinema. Double – even triple – bills were common, and many modern classics played on the midnight movie circuit for years, including Tobe Hooper's **Texas Chain Saw Massacre** (1974) and George Romero's **Night Of The Living Dead** (1968), alongside the work of John Waters and others.

3. John Waters, quoted in John G. Ives, *John Waters*, Thunder's Mouth Press, New York, 1992, p.88.

4. Selling out is a complex point, certainly the film is far more appetizing than Waters' previous works, but it received a PG-13 rating in America, as opposed to the lighter PG rating that **Hairspray** received. Further, the film enabled Waters to screen across the whole of the country, and not in isolated pockets.

5. Jack Stevenson, *Desperate Visions: The Films Of John Waters*, Creation Books, London, 1996, p.17.

6. John Waters, quoted in John G. Ives, *John Waters*, Thunder's Mouth Press, New York, 1992, p.90.

7. John Waters, quoted in John G. Ives, *John Waters*, Thunder's Mouth Press, New York, 1992, p.108.

8. John Waters, quoted in Stephen Rebello, "Johnny Handsome", *Movieline*, May, 1980.

9. Johnny Depp, in Mark Salisbury, ed, *Burton On Burton*, Faber And Faber, London, 1995, p.xi.

10. Johnny Depp, quoted in Christina Kelly, *Johnny Depp From A To W*, Sassy, May, 1990.

11. Johnny Depp, in Mark Salisbury, ed, *Burton On Burton*, p.xi.

12. John Waters, quoted in John G. Ives, *John Waters*, Thunder's Mouth Press, New York, 1992, p.75.

13. Johnny Depp, in Mark Salisbury, ed, *Burton On Burton*, p.ix.

14. John Waters quoted in V.Vale and Andrea Juno, eds, *Pranks: Re/Search 11*, Re/Search, 1987, p.120.

TAKING A SLICE OUT OF SUBURBIA: JOHNNY DEPP AS 'EDWARD SCISSORHANDS'

Edward Scissorhands (Tim Burton, 1990) is a modern day fairy tale of suburban dreams and nightmares. Cased in fairy tale imagery with heavy overtones of "Beauty And The Beast", the film also pulls heavily on the gothic genre. Reminiscent of Mary Shelley's gothic horror *Frankenstein* (1818) which foretold of the possible dehumanization brought about by the Industrial revolution[1], **Edward Scissorhands** is situated in a surreal 1950s suburbia, the spawning ground of modern day America's love/hate affair with its mass technological culture. The film offers above all, a kitsch, humorous and empathetic portrayal of the social outcast, with a resonance that reaches beyond the screen towards creators and audience alike.

Part fairy tale, part gothic romance[2], the film opens via the classic "doorway". Accompanied by angelic choir music the audience are led through a snow cloud into the castle home of Edward Scissorhands (a machine with a human appearance), past cobwebs, and labyrinthine staircases into the workshop of an inventor/father figure (Vincent Price). The inventor is overseeing a strange mechanical conveyor belt composed of machines who bear an uncanny resemblance to human beings who are incomplete/dismembered. The workshop has the appearance of a giant kitchen. The machines are involved in the production of childlike cut-out cookies (shaped like dogs, humans, and hearts). The inventor takes a heart-shaped cookie and holds it against one of the machines which appears to be chopping vegetables. This machine looks like the tin man minus facial features and a lower body (by implication this is Edward in embryonic form).

The film quickly moves into fairy tale mode as the snow wreathed hill-top castle is seen in long-shot through a suburban window. Inside an old lady (Winona Ryder)[3] begins to tell her grandchild a story: "I guess it would have to start with scissors... Once there was a man who had scissors for hands... A long time ago... incomplete and all alone..."

The old lady then opens the story of Edward Scissorhands as the film flashes back in time to a suburban landscape where all is neat and prescriptive. The houses are painted fairy tale bright pastel colours to create what Burton refers to as Edward's "slightly romanticized" view of the world. Filmed in Land O' Lakes, a four year-old settlement north of Tampa, Florida, Burton's team altered very little apart from the external house colours.

The film focuses on unsuccessful Avon Lady saleswoman Peg Boggs as she does the rounds of female neighbours, and then, as a last resort, drives over the ruined castle gate, and finds Edward hiding in the ruins of the castle attic. She calls out to him; "Hello, hello, why're you hiding back there? You don't have to be afraid of me, I'm Peg Boggs your local Avon representative and I'm as harmless as cherry pie". Peg coaxes Edward from the shadows. Edward has enormous scissor hands, wears a black leather bondage bodysuit, has tangled black hair, and a white face with large scars. Peg is shocked by his appearance, Edward explains; "I'm not finished". He tells Peg that his parent, the inventor, "didn't wake up". The inventor died before Edward's human form could be completed. Edward's humanity arises from an unexplained and magical source and is representative of a spiritual rather than material origin. Peg's maternal and cosmetic-instructor instincts are stirred. She tells Edward that she will take him home to live with her family, and that she knows a doctor who may be able to help, along with the power of her modern day bible, "The Big Avon Handbook".

Edward enters the home of Peg, husband Bill (Alan Arkin), son Kevin (Robert Oliveri), and daughter Kim (Winona Ryder), a cliché of the all-American family with bowling champ dad, clever son, and golden prom queen daughter. He soon attracts attention, particularly that of the neighbourhood women whose ringleader Joyce is a stereotypical nymphomaniac housewife (Kathy Bates), her long manicured nails which she taps impatiently echoing Edward's carefully controlled scissored hands. Local organ player and Christian fanatic Esmerelda (O-Lan Jones) refers to Edward as "satan... a perversion of nature" (which enthrals Joyce). Esmerelda accuses Peg, in fairy tale fashion, of having "strayed from the path". Kevin refers to Edward as a "Freak" and Kim is irritated by his presence in her space. Edward soon begins to exert "scissor-hand" skills, creating a topiary dinosaur and a topiary Boggs family grouping.

At this point the film flashes back to Edward's life with the inventor. Edward is seen dressed like a romantic fairy tale hero with neat hair, listening as the inventor instructs him from a book of etiquette, and then encourages Edward to laugh by reciting a limerick. Edward appears as a young Renaissance man who is being groomed for a high place in society. Joyce, unable to bear not having closer contact with Edward invites the neighbourhood to a barbecue at the Boggs house. Edward, like a true mother's helper, speedily chops the salad for the barbecue (recalling his kitchen-machine/workshop origins). At the barbecue the local men attempt to jest with Edward, and one says "I have a doctor friend of mine, might be able to help you". A war vet tells Edward that he's not handicapped, implying that he is, enforcing social roles of exclusion. The women crowd around Edward and take it turns to mother him, spoon feed him. Joyce however has

a more sexual agenda, she is fascinated by Edward's "cutting" power, and "mysterious" attributes; whether he has "hot or cold hands?".

The narrative then returns to suburbia and introduces Jim (Anthony Michael Hall), Kim's bullish jock boyfriend. Jim is an unpleasant bully with extreme authoritarian parents. Jim dislikes Edward, particularly when Edward's skills and easy going nature begins to win the admiration of Kim. Edward becomes a creative hairstylist to the neighbourhood women and their pet dogs, leading to an appearance on a local chat show where once again someone tells him: "I know a doctor who may be able to help you". The chat show ends in turmoil when Edward accidentally causes an electrical explosion by cutting the microphone cable, but not before he has made virtual contact with Kim who is sitting at home watching TV with Jim. An audience member asks if he has a girlfriend and Edward stares penetratingly at the camera into the watching eyes of Kim.

Joyce tries to further her relationship with Edward by opening a beauty salon with him, "Shear Heaven". She attempts to seduce Edward in the prospective salon. Edward flees in terror and naively tells the Boggs family about Joyce. Bill however, is only interested in the financial arrangements of the relationship. He sees Edward as fulfilling the American Dream of the self-made man who unlike him and their suburban neighbours has the courage to escape the mass identity of corporate America. Bill: "There's nothing like running your own business, I've never done it myself, but from what I gather it's the greatest pleasure a working man can have".

However the American Dream, whether desired or not, turns sour for Edward at this point. The neighbourhood collectively turns against Edward. Joyce spreads rumours of attempted rape and the rest of the women follow her. Edward is knowingly tricked by Kim at Jim's request into breaking and entering Jim's parents' house so that Jim can afford to buy himself a "love van". Edward is arrested and held in custody and takes all the blame for the crime. Peg and Bill like true armchair moralists believe that all depraved behaviour is piped from outside their communities into their homes via TV; "Damn those TV programs... Damn them all to Hell". The local police sergeant (Rex Fox) is concerned that Edward is too vulnerable and generous to live in society, unlike the police psychologist who feels that Edward is an imaginative and amoral character whose "awareness of what we call reality is radically underdeveloped". Edward later tells Kim that he knew it was wrong but did it "Because you asked me to".

The Boggs family rally round, Bill tries to teach Edward social morals of right and wrong, but both Edward and Kim express a belief in more heartfelt morals. However the annual Boggs' Christmas party is planned. Edward prepares an ice sculpture of Kim as she dances beneath him in the resultant ice flurries. Jim arrives in a fury, and shouts at Edward who

accidentally cuts Kim's hand. Jim calls him a "ghoul, freak" who "can't touch anything without destroying it", and tells him to get the "Hell out" of suburbia. Jim and Kim argue. Jim: "Are you nuts?... Are you serious, lose you to *that*, he's not even human". Jim tries to convince Kim that Edward was trying to hurt her. Kim, unimpressed by this manipulative display of macho posturing tells Jim to go, she doesn't love him any more.

Meanwhile Edward is tearing up suburbia, ripping off the clothes that Peg had given him, dismembering his topiary hedges, and slashing car tyres. In a magically comic scene, Esmerelda is seen thumping out hymns on her home organ, when she is distracted by the sound of snipping; she moves to her window and recoils in horror – Edward has left her a "demonic hedge" with red fairy light eyes as a parting gift. The neighbourhood form a lynch mob with Esmerelda chanting "demon... demon".

Peg tells Kim that she will try and find Edward who should return to the castle, "because at least he's safe and we can just go back to normal". Edward meanwhile is seen sheltering beneath a giant teddy bear topiary hedge, and with empathy he trims the facial fur from a shaggy neighbourhood dog so that it can see. He sees a police car and flees to the house. Kim asks Edward to hold her, he does so with her help, he is unable to have a complete relationship with another human being because of his scissor hands.

Edward's incomplete form and relationship to others is enforced by a flashback to the inventor's workshop. The inventor lovingly hands Edward a "present", he holds out two human-shaped hands for Edward to inspect. Edward is enthraled, he kisses the fingertips of one of the hands and fails to notice that the inventor is slipping out of life before him. Edward stakes the hands in an effort to prevent the inventor from falling to the ground. The attempt fails and both his surrogate father and his longed for hands smash to the floor. Edward is helpless without them. He attempts to caress the inventor's face, but causes a deep cut and blood coats his scissor hands.

Back in suburbia Jim is drunk, he crudely tells his friend Denny (John McMahon) about Kim and Edward, "Forget holding her hand, picture the damage he could do in other places". He then bullies the drunken Denny into driving Denny's van to track Edward down. The neighbourhood lynch mentality has also reached fever pitch. Kevin is harassed by the local war vet who wants to hear news of Edward's chase. Kevin is sickened and scared, Kevin hurries home and walks into the path of the drunken Denny's van. Edward sees this in time, rescues Kevin but unfortunately cuts him in the process. The neighbours crowd round and Peg tries to rescue Edward but Jim uses Kevin's injury as an excuse to beat up on Edward. Edward slashes Jim's arm in self-defence and Kim tells him to "run".

The police sergeant who was previously concerned about Edward follows him in his patrol car at a leisurely pace with the neighbourhood marching behind. Five gunshots are then heard coming from the entrance to the castle and the sergeant instructs Edward to hide, "Go on, run". The townsfolk arrive and he tells them that it's all over, to go home, then leaves. Joyce however is not satisfied, she wants blood, and she leads the townsfolk through the gates. Kim meanwhile has run ahead and finds Edward in the castle attic. Jim surprises them and shoots at Edward, it misses and hits the roof which collapses on Edward. Jim, like the true coward he is, beats Edward while he is held down by the roof debris. Kim hits Jim and threatens to kill him by taking hold of one of Edward's scissor hands. Jim slaps her, cutting her with the scissor hand in the process. Edward tries to help Kim but Jim warns him off. Edward reaches his tolerance level and stabs Jim in the stomach, he falls backward through the attic window, landing dead in the garden below as Edward and Kim look on. Kim and Edward kiss and say good-bye. She takes a spare scissors hand hanging from the wall, tells Edward that she loves him and confronts the townsfolk below. Holding the hand high she tells the crowd: "They killed each other". The mob leaves.

The fairy tale concludes; granny Kim tells her grandchild that she never saw Edward again, and prefers not to see him now because, "I'm an old woman now, I would rather he remembered me the way I was". She knows that Edward is still alive by virtue of the snow which began to stream down to suburbia after Edward had returned to the castle. The film cuts to Edward in his attic home creating Disney-style, Snow White ice sculpture of birdbaths, children at play, and a sculpture of Kim dancing in the snow; and snow is seen puffing from the attic window. The film flashes back to Kim as a girl dancing, then shows a long-shot of the castle in snow flurries, fading out to white and then black.

Edward Scissorhands is Depp's most successful starring commercial film to date, grossing over $56 million. However commercial success was not the sole factor that dominated either Depp or director Tim Burton. If box office success had been the overall motive then Tom Cruise, who had initially been up for the role of Edward, would surely have been chosen. According to industry gossip[4] Cruise would have only been prepared to play the role if Edward's facial scars of social ostracism had been obliterated by the film's end. Depp wore these outcast scars with pride, like his much-famed tattoos. Fully committed to his role, Depp endured much discomfort; Winona Ryder has said that: "During shooting days in Florida, when temperatures soared above 110 degrees, he stayed trussed up in Edward's black leather body suit without complaint"[5].

Caroline Thompson comments: "Johnny Depp and Tim Burton have marvellous senses of humour. They both see the world as a very absurd place. They're not unique in that, but they share a way of looking at it. It is clear to me that Tim has chosen Johnny as the reflection of himself on screen"[6]. Burton holds a slightly different view, "the film is not autobiographical, because it was important for me to be as objective as possible. That's why I felt very lucky to have Johnny because he brought to it a lot of themes that are nearer his life which, when I started to talk to him, I liked very much. I could look at him and draw upon his world in a way[7]". Depp's and Burton's relationship was one of sharing. Johnny Depp has great admiration for Tim Burton. He says that he felt like "a loser, an outcast" when Tim Burton came along and "rescued him"[8]. Depp says of Burton: "I have never seen someone so obviously out of place fit right in his way"[9].

The idea for **Edward Scissorhands** came from Burton; "The idea came from a drawing I did a long time ago... It came subconsciously and was linked to character who wants to touch but can't, who was both creative and destructive – those sort of contradictions can create a kind of ambivalence. It was very much linked to a feeling. The manifestation of the image made itself apparent and probably came to the surface when I was a teenager, because it's a very teenage thing. It had to do with relationships. I just felt I couldn't communicate. It was the feeling that your image and the how people perceive you are at odds with what is inside you, which is a fairly common feeling. I think a lot of people feel that way to some degree, because it's frustrating and sad to feel a certain way but for it not to come through. So the idea had to do with image and perception. I remember growing up and feeling that there is not a lot of room for acceptance. You are taught at a very early age to conform... from day one you're categorized. This was the strongest impulse in the film"[10].

Burton's films all share this theme of social exclusion, and often use fairy tale elements in order to show a distorted reality that underlies the ordered exterior of suburban life, an environment which Burton himself experienced growing up in suburban Burbank. Often critical, but sometimes presenting an ideal, his films seek to expose repressed desires, to show the "Sexual stuff. There's a certain kind of kinkiness to suburbia"[11]. Burton's films show the darker side of suburbia; "the parallel between suburban life and a horror movie was closer than you might think. The mob mentality is in a lot of these horror movies". Depp also grew up in suburban neighbourhoods although his family were constantly on the move, and he shares Burton's imagination and strong desire to escape conformity and side with the outcast. Both have found Hollywood to be constrictive; Burton states: "Hollywood is so strange... for a community made up of so many freakish outsiders, it's oddly conservative"[12]. For his three previous films, Burton had worked with Warners but the studio didn't take to the idea of **Edward Scissorhands**, so Burton was happy to work Twentieth Century-Fox under the directorship of Joe Roth, who enabled him greater freedom.

Depp also finds that success can still lead to feelings of ostracism; "Success is a strange word, y'know. It started making me feel even more freakish, even more weird. More – y'know, more outside"[13]. Tim Burton felt that these feelings link Johnny Depp to Edward:

"In America, Johnny is very much known as a teen idol and he's perceived as difficult and aloof; there are all sorts of things written about him in the press that are completely untrue... he's perceived as dark and difficult and weird, and is judged by his looks. But he's almost completely the opposite of this perception. So the themes of Edward, of image and perception, of somebody being perceived to be the opposite of what he is, was a theme he could relate to. The words 'freakish' and 'freak' have so many interpretations, and in a weird way he sort of relates to freaks because he's treated as one. That flip-flopping and inverting of themes and perceptions was something he totally responded to because he goes through that all the time. You pick up a tabloid and he's portrayed as the brooding James Dean type or whatever way people want to label him as, but he's not. People get judged by their looks a lot... It's sad when you're judged by the way you look, and that sadness builds up inside in you because, at least for me, there was always a desire to connect with people – not everybody, but

some people, one or two – and he's probably been through a lot of that kind of stuff... I think a lot of the character is him. He has this kind of naive quality which as you get older gets tested and has holes poked into it. It's hard to maintain that, because you don't want to shield yourself from society and the rest of the world completely, but at the same time you'd like to maintain a certain kind of openness and feeling that you had earlier on in your life. And I would imagine Johnny is somebody who would want to protect that to some degree"[14].

Depp was sent the script for **Edward Scissorhands** in the winter of 1989 by his agent Tracey Jacobs. At the time he was a teen-idol, playing Tom Hanson, an undercover high school cop on Fox's *21 Jump Street*, a role which Depp was only happy with when he felt that it dealt realistically with teen problems. Depp was also in the process of starring as Wade "Cry Baby" Walker in director John Waters' kitsch melodrama **Cry-Baby**. Waters told Depp that he could kill his teen-idol image by completely overplaying it.

Depp was completely taken with the script, a meeting was set up with Burton and co-producer Denise Di Novi in the coffee shop of the Bel Age hotel in Los Angeles. Depp immediately felt that Tim Burton was closely identified with his fictional character, "This mad sensitive madman is Edward

Scissorhands". However, Depp felt unconfident about convincing Burton that he was ideal for the role:

"...that I was Edward, that I knew him inside and out... I was sure we could work well together and I was positive, if given the chance, I could carry out his artistic vision for **Edward Scissorhands**. My chances were at best slim – if that. Better known people than me were not only being considered for the role but battling, fighting, kicking, screaming, begging for it. Only one director had really stuck his neck out for me and that was John Waters, a great outlaw film-maker, a man Tim and I had huge respect and admiration for. John had taken a chance on me to spoof my 'given' image in **Cry-Baby**. But would Tim see something in me that would make him take the risk?"[15].

Burton did take a risk. He hadn't seen *21 Jump Street*, but he had seen a picture of him and liked his eyes, especially in relation to Edward's character; "We wanted him right from the beginning..."[16]. Burton also approached John Waters and viewed the "dailies" of **Cry-Baby** in private while it was being shot. Depp was ecstatic to be chosen for the role, it released him from his existence as "TV boy".

"This role was freedom. Freedom to create, experiment, learn and exorcize something in me. Rescued from the world of mass-product, bang-'em out TV death by this odd, brilliant young guy who had spent his youth drawing strange pictures, stomping around the soup-bowl of Burbank, feeling quite freakish himself ...Resuscitated from my jaded views of 'Hollyweird' and what it's like to not have any control of what you really want for yourself. In essence, I owe the majority of whatever success I've been lucky enough to have to that one weird, wired meeting with Tim. Because if it weren't for him, I think I would have gone ahead... and quit that fucking show while I still had some semblance of integrity left. And I also believe that because of Tim's belief in me, Hollywood opened its doors, playing a strange follow-the-leader game."[17]

Burton defines the evolution of Edward's character: "First came the image, linked to those feelings of not being accepted. Then from that came the images of the ice and the hedges, just as a natural outgrowth of him being a helpful, handy household item"[18]. Depp was completely drawn to playing Edward; "It was bizarre 'cos there was a freedom, a kind of safety, in being that open and that unguarded. And that was... For me, that was a lot of me in that role, Scissorhands. I identified absolutely, totally, completely with Edward Scissorhands"[19].

Edward is a social outcast, he wears black leather, a classic film signifier of the outsider. His pasty white facial make-up and tangled black hair contrive to give him the appearance of a walking voodoo doll. Yet Edward is not a James Dean or Marlon Brando character – he is not a black leather-jacketed rebel. He is perhaps closer to Depp's literary/life heroes embodied in the work of J.D. Salinger and especially Jack Kerouac. He has a childlike presence, he is in effect a child in adult form. He lacks all sexual aggression, it has been displaced to his scissor hands. Edward is an orphaned child who is unable to care for himself, his castle home is gradually crumbling. The castle's garden is full of topiary animals/toys and appears as a nursery garden. Peg Boggs' first instinct towards Edward is maternal. Depp played on this vulnerability in Edward's character; "He had this unconditional love... this totally pure, completely open character, the sweetest thing in the world, whose appearance is incredibly dangerous – until you get a look at his eyes. I missed Edward when I was done. I really miss him."[20]

Edward is a champion of the underdog. Depp has also emulated this in various forms in his own life, not perhaps by being a social outcast, but by acting out the uncompromised rehabilitation of the social outcast. His career shows a tension between being a potential outcast and a scepticism towards success and the trappings of fame. Both are extreme positions which pull strongly on feelings of empowerment and disempowerment, and both entail a sense of isolation which Edward's character embodies. Edward has great creative powers but these powers can also be destructive, his hands can be lethal weapons, but their real harm becomes unintentionally self-directed, as seen by his facial scars and isolation. Edward cannot obtain a middle ground where he fits neatly into mainstream culture – a space which Burton's films show as being deceptive, unobtainable, and ultimately undesirable.

Depp says of the roles that he has played: "They're outsiders. They're people society says aren't normal, and I think you have to stand up for people like that. But I didn't plan it... I love Edward. He was total honesty. Honesty is what matters, and I have an absurd fascination with it..."[21]

One of the most striking things about Depp's performance as Edward, is the versatile range of expression that he gives to the mainly silent and fearful character. Edward is a gentle character, misunderstood through his appearance and unusual behaviour. He is not a gothic monster, that role is reserved for suburbia and its regime of mass identification which creates underlying anxieties. The real violence and blind anger comes from inside the community and is directed at the outsider. Edward only kills Jim when he realizes that he will stop at nothing, including harming Kim to bring about his downfall. Edward in fact appears as the most feeling and humane character in the film. Burton puts this strength of expression down to Depp's ability to act with his eyes, one of the features that struck him when he met Depp: "I like people's eyes a lot and, especially with a character like this who doesn't really speak, eyes are very important"[22]. Burton comments on this ability:

"I remember Johnny was able to do something that amazed me. I was very close to him one day, watching him doing a scene, and the next day we saw it on film, and almost without doing anything he was able to do something with his eyes that made them glassy. It was if he was about to cry, like one of those Walter Keane paintings with the big eyes. I don't know how he did it. It wasn't something we did with the camera or the lighting, it was incredible..."[23]

Depp's use of posture and movement is a constant reminder of Edward's machine status, he utilizes small effects like letting the scissor hands hang down like the paws of a dog (emphasizing submission and reprimand). Like many gestures this could appear as sickly sentimental but Depp manages to bring a dignity to the character. Terry Gilliam, who directed Depp in **Fear And Loathing In Las Vegas** has said of Depp: "You begin to think that Johnny's a silent movie star, is what he really is, and he just happens to be born a little bit late. He has the same kind of skills as a Buster Keaton or a Charlie Chaplin has; they use their entire being"[24]. Depp believes "that everything is in the eyes and in the body language... if it's honest in the eyes and in the body and in the movement – then it's there [...] What the silent guys were able to say with their eyes, or with a tilt of the head – the way they'd turn their head or something – they could say everything. They didn't need words"[25].

Edward was the first major film role Depp had played that departed from any conventional teen heart-throb, although arguably the character has a passive sexuality which mirrors that of other teen-idols such as "boy-band" characters. However, following on from **Cry-Baby** it seemed to be quite a radical departure. Terry Gillian describes this transition: "I saw Edward Scissorhands and he first appears with a terrible fright wig on, and he's got pasty makeup, and you think 'Oh this is a joke. This is never going to work'. And within ten, fifteen minutes I totally believed the character. Now that's an extraordinary talent: to take such extreme characters who are cartoons or grotesques – things that maybe would almost work better on the stage – and he's able to bring them into a naturalistic world of cinema and make them work."[26]

John Waters describes Depp as an "auteur actor" who seeks less mainstream directors and scripts because they enable him to take greater risks and maintain some control over his career in creative terms. Depp is aware that the movie business remains first and foremost as a commercial industry; "It's probably ridiculous the way I talk about honesty and shit when really, to what am I being true? Some company. A bunch of guys who invest in a movie... That's not so pure. It's art and commerce, oil and water"[27]. Yet Depp does seek to push at Hollywood's creative boundaries, believing that the "movie-going audience would like to see something different... the Hollywood studio system has under-estimated them..."[28]

Edward Scissorhands *has* something which is a little different – a cut above the rest.

NOTES

1. Mary Shelley's *Frankenstein* has a strong "reproductive" theme, which speculates on the reproduction/continuation of society but also on the more basic question of maternity. Mary had herself lost a daughter who was born prematurely just over a year before she wrote her novel, she also had a son who was less than five months old. Interestingly, Caroline Thompson, (Associate producer, screenwriter, and co-author of **Edward Scissorhands**), had previously written *First Born*, a novel about an abortion that comes back to life.

2. Popular genres question the human condition, in veiled terms they are asking; "What does it mean to be human?". This question is directed at a particular society, often in response to a period of socio-economic change such as those created by technological/scientific advances whose effects can alter the way that people live. Projected selves or "others" are created in order that this question can be interrogated. These "others" allow for the strengthening of self-definition by providing a compare and contrast relationship to the self. Genres which very obviously distort reality can critique society, but these fantastical, distorted creatures (representative of what can't be seen or described within reality) are also depoliticized by nature of their unreal appearance. The gothic genre is more critical than the fairy tale genre because the relationship between human self and "other" remains fairly clear. **Edward Scissorhands** is a gothic romance framed, and coloured by a fairy tale formula. This allows the audience to identify with its central outcast character while accepting that a story is about to be told and belief needs to be suspended.

3. Depp and Ryder were a couple at this point.

4. See Bill Zehme, "Sweet Sensation", *Rolling Stone*, 1.10.91.

5. Ibid,.

6. Sibley, Adrian (dir./producer), "What's Eating Johnny Depp?". Channel Four/Mentorn Barraclough Carey, 1998.

7. Salisbury, Mark; (ed.), *Burton On Burton*, Faber and Faber, London, 1995, p91.

8. Ibid, pxii.

9. Ibid,.

10. Ibid, p87.

11. Ibid. p90.

12. Ibid. p84.

13. "What's Eating Johnny Depp?".

14. *Burton On Burton*, p91–2.

15. Ibid, pxi.

16. Ibid, p91.

17. Ibid. pxi–xii.

18. Ibid, p89–1.

19. "What's Eating Johnny Depp?".

20. *Rolling Stone*.

21. See Kevin Cook, "Playboy Interview: Johnny Depp", *Playboy* 1996.

22. *Burton On Burton*, p91.

23. Ibid, p94.

24. "What's Eating Johnny Depp?".

25. Ibid,.

26. Ibid,.

27. *Playboy*.

28. "What's Eating Johnny Depp?".

GOING NOWHERE: 'WHAT'S EATING GILBERT GRAPE?'

"I come from Des Moines, Iowa. Someone has to."
–Bill Bryson, "The Lost Continent"

Johnny Depp's fractured upbringing in Kentucky, and his later move to small-town Florida were perfect preparation for **What's Eating Gilbert Grape?**, a film about family loyalty, transience and the ultimate possibility of "escape" to a better life. Like Juliette Lewis' "worldly kind of girl" Becky, Depp's early family life revolved around frequent uprooting and house-hopping, and, as with Gilbert, he was forced into the role of unlikely patriarch following parental break-up and his mother's depression. Having just made a film about an outsider's acceptance into a tight community (**Edward Scissorhands**), Depp turned to the flipside: the troubles of feeling trapped inside the community, struggling with a swelling fascination for the unknown.

The film opens with Gilbert and his retarded brother Arnie (Leonardo DiCaprio) loitering at the roadside in anticipation of the yearly "parade" of holidaymakers in their camper-vans. Arnie repeatedly asks when they're coming, Gilbert repeatedly says they'll be coming soon, and then they come, and Arnie gives chase, squealing with delight. Gilbert's voice-over explains that the camper-vans have the right idea – just passing through.

Gilbert and Arnie live with mother Bonnie and sisters Amy and Ellen, in rural Endora, a town which, says Gilbert, trying to describe it is "like dancing to no music – it's a town where nothing much happens and nothing much ever will". Gilbert works at the local grocery store, and his boss, Mr Lamson, is concerned at his customers succumbing to the commercial lures of out-of-town supermarket Foodland ("It's those lobsters in the tank, isn't it?"). Gilbert makes deliveries in his van and we learn that he's involved in an affair with one of his customers, Mrs Carver, and that her insurance company boss husband seems to suspect.

At home, Gilbert is the glue that has held the family together since his father's suicide several years ago. Sister Ellen is spiteful and adolescent, but older Amy is more stable. Arnie is erratic and lively, about to turn eighteen, having originally only been given ten years to live at the most. Bonnie weighs five-hundred pounds and hasn't left the house for seven years. She's physically unable to climb the stairs and spends most of her time sitting and sleeping on the vast, winded sofa, being attended by the others. Local kids are fascinated by her and queue to catch a glimpse through the living-

room window. Gilbert, dismissive of his mother's condition, often gives them a leg-up, to the dismay of local handyman Tucker (John C. Reilly). But Gilbert is fiercely protective of Arnie, who frequently takes to climbing the town water tower and, as most of the population gather for the cabaret, Gilbert talks him down, assuring the sheriff that this is definitely the last time. Arnie occasionally spins into distressed reveries at Gilbert's assurances ("We're not going anywhere! We're not going anywhere!")

Tucker and Gilbert join the morbid town undertaker Bobby (Crispin Glover) for a chat over the minutiae of their respective lives. Tucker talks of his desire to take charge of a "Burger Barn" franchise and asks Gilbert how his mother is. "She's fat", he replies. Bobby is depressed because business is slow ("Nobody's dying"), and enthralls his friends with stories of how he relieves boredom by "joking around" with some of his uglier corpses. Gilbert is distracted by the sight of Becky (Juliette Lewis), a young girl travelling with her grandmother whose camper-van has broken down on the edge of town. Becky and Gilbert spend time together. She says she'd like to meet his mother. He says, no she wouldn't. Becky explains that she moves around a lot following her parents' break-up a few years ago. Gilbert: "We don't really move. My momma's kind of attached to the house."

Following a thwarted seduction, Mrs Carver confesses to Gilbert that she could have taken any guy in town for her lover, but she chose him: "I knew you'd always be there. I knew you'd never leave." Later, Mr Carver dies after drowning in the kiddy-pool following a cardiac arrest, and the death sets the whole town buzzing with suspicion. Gilbert can barely contain his relief when a part acquired for Becky's grandmother's car fails to get it started again, and Becky, Gilbert and Arnie go to the local lake, where Gilbert is finally urged into the water. But, Arnie slips away and climbs the water tower again. This time, Gilbert can't stop the sheriff taking him in.

Bonnie rages against the insensitivity of the police and, to the family's amazement, demands to be taken into town. They drive to the station in a comically lop-sided car, where Bonnie thunders down the hall and demands Arnie's release. Of course, most of the town turn up for the freakshow and it's a long, undignified walk back to the car. Becky tells Gilbert that she's leaving tomorrow, and Arnie finally invites her to his eighteenth birthday party.

Back home, Arnie runs wild and ruins the birthday cake. Gilbert is forced to go to Foodland to buy another, where he's spotted by his boss. Later, Arnie raids the fridge and Gilbert flips, beating him before running to his van and driving out of Endora. Arnie runs to Becky, who looks after him before sending him home. Gilbert turns round and comes back to Becky, where he tells her about his father: "He was just there. You'd try to get him to smile, to laugh, to get mad... nothing. It was like he was already dead."

The two sleep out in the open and, in the morning, Gilbert goes home to make up with Arnie and Bonnie, who tells him she was afraid he wouldn't come back ("I never meant to be like this. I never wanted to be a joke."). Becky arrives and Gilbert finally introduces her to his reluctant mother.

Becky leaves and Bonnie hauls herself up to her bed for the first time in years, where she dies in her sleep. Amy is worried about the inevitable crowd that will turn out to see her mother air-lifted from the house. Gilbert goes down to the basement (the scene of his father's suicide) and smashes the supports and rafters ("I'm not gonna let her be a joke"). He directs the family in clearing the house of furniture before setting it alight. One year on, after explaining about Amy and Ellen's situation, Gilbert and Arnie wait by the roadside again, but this time one of the camper-vans stops and they're picked up by Becky and her grandmother.

"I figure Johnny knew a lot about Gilbert. I think he studied this kind of guy closely."
–Director Lasse Hallstrom.[1]

The traditional cinematic approach to small-town American life is a fixation with the dark undercurrents ebbing below the middle-class surface simplicity (David Lynch has practically made a career from tales of supernatural and criminal depravity beyond the picket-fences and lawn-sprinklers). **What's Eating Gilbert Grape?** prefers to zoom in on the basic humanities of life: the persistent boredom and short-termism, the appetite for simple excitement.

What's Eating Gilbert Grape? was directed by Lasse Hallstrom, a low-key Swede renowned for his touch with tender family stories (**My Life As A Dog, Once Around**). The screenplay was adapted by Iowan novelist Peter Hedges, from his own book of the same name, partly based on his own childhood. Hedges' father was overweight, and he was forced into the role of primary carer to his younger brother. Hedges used a dedication in the paperback edition to confirm the fiction-reality issue ("To my mother, who is not fat, and my father, who is not dead.") The screenplay's initial focus was the relationship between Becky and Gilbert, but the performances from DiCaprio as Arnie and newcomer Darlene Cates as Bonnie shifted the balance of the story onto the Grape family itself.

Hedges had written Bonnie as a minor role with barely any lines, little more than a lurking presence at the centre of the Grape household. But Cates, recruited from a Sally Jessy Raphael show ("Too Heavy To Leave The House") turned out to be a fine actress, and her screen-time was expanded. Although Cates was honoured to be given the part, she was uncomfortable with the impression that Bonnie doesn't bathe and the way the floors creak

when she walks around the house. Hallstrom, however, insisted that the dilapidated feel of the house was essential to the feel of the uneasy family unit. He was also keen to cast Depp, noting his naturally compassionate demeanour and relevant life history.

A then-unknown Leonardo DiCaprio was given the role of Arnie despite Hallstrom's initial concern that his looks wouldn't sit convincingly with the character's nature. DiCaprio studied videos of mentally retarded teenagers, absorbing subtle mannerisms and eventually creating some of his own. His agent persuaded him to take the part, insisting, against DiCaprio's instincts, that the film would be a success. It was, and DiCaprio was rightly Oscar-nominated for bringing a tangible sense of difficult likability to Arnie; he's not cloyingly overcooked for our sympathies. We see why he's hard to live with, but also why the family choose to live with him. When the film was finished, it was DiCaprio's Oscar nomination which saved it from obscurity. Paramount encountered difficulty getting theatres (particularly those in the mid-west) to show it at all. It played in only six cities in Minnesota and was about to be canned, when the nomination was announced.

For Depp, the film expanded his profile which, bizarrely, following **Edward Scissorhands**, was teetering dangerously close to teeny heart-throb again (the set was constantly buzzed by autograph-junkies). Ironically, the poster-boy mantle would soon be passed to DiCaprio. Modelling his

appearance on childhood friend Bones, Depp dyed his hair red and had his teeth bonded and chipped into snaggles, reasoning that Gilbert wouldn't have had the money to fix them and, anyway, wouldn't have cared. Given the material's resonance with his early years, Depp found the role difficult: "Sometimes you play roles that are close to you, you identify with the guy. Not that you 'become' the person, because I don't buy into that shit at all, but this movie was a rough time for me. I poisoned myself constantly: drinking, didn't eat right, no sleep, lots of cigarettes. It was a really lonely time."[2]

Becky: "Tell me what you want as fast as it comes to you."
Gilbert: "I want to be a good person."

Gilbert's meeting with Becky proves a strong catalyst to his nagging feelings of escapism. Practically everyone in the film has their own flavour of wanderlust: Arnie with the water tower, Mrs Carver and her illicit desires for Gilbert, Tucker with his need to move to a more prosaic level of independence with his burger business. Becky's admission of being "worldly" stems, as with Depp, from an unsettled upbringing. "We'd go from neighbourhood to neighbourhood," says Depp. "Sometimes from one house to the house next door. I don't know why. My mom would get ants somehow. There's a huge history of my family out there: furniture, my toys, schoolwork... everything was abandoned, left in attics or garages – all gone." Becky and Gilbert's needs dovetail: she, bounced from mother to father, yearns for a kind of emotional stability, while he, stagnant, desires discovery and expression. Gilbert's life is little more than a roll-call of unquestioned responsibilities: Bonnie, Arnie, his job. Becky provides a channel of blessed unpredictability, and his keenness to introduce her to his mother implies a need for approval to seek an independent emotional life.

Far from being mawkishly represented as a standard "unfortunate", Arnie is Gilbert's surrogate voice. He flatly tells Becky that she's not invited to his party, Gilbert apologises for him, but Becky is touched by his uncomplicated honesty. Later, Arnie fumbles her groceries and Gilbert can't apologise enough. Again, Becky is irritated by the contrition: she's not sorry, Arnie's not sorry, so who is Gilbert apologising for?

Becky is instrumental in Gilbert's key transition: the way he moves from reactive to active. He lights other people's cigarettes, delivers other people's groceries, dutifully responds to Mrs Carver's sexual advances. But Becky encourages him to think – and act – creatively. As the two sit together and watch the sunset, Becky remarks how the sky is fascinating because it's so "limitless". Gilbert merely responds by agreeing that yes, it is "big". Becky chastises him, arguing that "big" is a lazy word and he has to think of something less passive, more expansive. By the time Gilbert attacks Arnie, he's reached his pass-over point, but can't follow through to drive away from town, to "disappear", as his father had done. Instead, he returns with added compassion for his mother, and, after she climbs the stairs to die with dignity, she and Gilbert share what is virtually a death-bed scene. Bonnie tells him he's her "knight in glittering armour". Gilbert corrects her: "I thought it was 'shining' armour." No, says Bonnie. He doesn't shine, he glitters: hinting at something more complex than straight carer. Following her death, after Amy's worry about the grim spectacle of Bonnie being removed from the house, Gilbert takes ultimate control: banishing his father's memory by trashing the basement before preparing the house as his mother's funeral pyre. The passage is complete: his mother and father are over, Mrs Carver is over, his job is over (after being spotted by his boss at Foodland), and Arnie has turned eighteen. Now, he can finally leave town.

There's a minor debate about the question-mark in the film's title. With: a more abstract enquiry into Gilbert's restless, reflective nature. Without: a stark round-up of the obvious external forces edging him ever nearer to the final escape. It is, of course, Endora itself that's eating/destroying Gilbert Grape: the sheer emptiness of a place so bland it's not worth describing – a place where, as Depp himself has said of Miramar, "you were just... there." In the end, escape isn't achieved out of abandonment or recklessness, but from a logical, humane reaction to the closure of family commitment caused by Bonnie's death. Becky's meeting with Bonnie is pivotal, as Gilbert finally transfers the suffocating love of his mother to the hope of a more nourishing, mutual life with Becky.

"I would hope that people might view their fellow beings, all beings, with more empathy, more compassion, with a desire to understand. Even if they can't know why people are the way they are, to understand that they're probably that way for a good reason."
–Peter Hedges, screenwriter/novelist, **What's Eating Gilbert Grape?**

NOTES

1. *GQ*, October 1993.

2. *GQ*, October 1993.

CELEBRATING THE OUTSIDERS:
TIM BURTON'S 'ED WOOD'

1.

Tim Burton's bio-pic **Ed Wood** focuses on the most legendary of "Z Grade" auteurs, Edward D. Wood Jr. The director, producer and writer behind such classics as **Glen Or Glenda** (1953 – note that Wood cast himself as the transvestite lead role under the name Daniel Davis), **Bride Of The Monster** (1955), **Plan 9 From Outer Space** (1959), and **The Sinister Urge** (1961). Ed Wood's films have entered contemporary cinematic history under the spurious banner of "the worst movies ever made", a title originally bestowed on them as a result of the pages of the ultimately ignorant and condescending *The Golden Turkey Awards* by the writers Michael and Harry Medved.

Wood's movies earned this title primarily because of their strange plotting and apparently careless *mise-en-scène*, manifested most clearly in **Plan 9 From Outer Space**, during sequences where night and day are intercut, seemingly at random, and against any recognizable dominant notions of cinematic verisimilitude or narrative coherence. As Jim Morton has observed, Wood's cinematic aesthetic – largely driven by poverty and make-do-necessity – results in a style that is almost akin to Dada[1]. To condemn, or condescendingly laugh knowingly, at these imagined cinematic *faux pas*, as the Medveds would have their readers do, fails to recognize the very energy and pure passion that was the motivation for Wood's vision. The cinematic power inherent in Wood's movies comes from the director's clear pleasure in telling stories and making movies regardless of the traditional constraints imposed by the ultimately stupefying aesthetic criteria celebrated by the (generally) monotonous works produced by the major Hollywood studios. In Hollywood's so-called classic period, Wood sought to pursue his own visions regardless of his limited budgets. He often shot a scene only once, and utilized whatever sets and props he could, and employed largely unskilled casts that included such legendary non-actors as the gigantic Swedish wrestler Tor Johnson, late night TV gothic-horror hostess Vampira, and celebrity psychic Criswell[2]. One of the few professional actors with whom Wood worked was Bela Lugosi – deemed as washed-up because of an addiction to morphine and methadone by the studios and industry – and Wood recognized Bela as a true great and became close friends with the elderly actor.

Amongst Wood's main influences were comic books, film and radio serials, pulp novels, genre pictures – horror and science fiction – especially **Dracula** (Tod Browning, 1930), which had a lasting impact on the youthful

Edward. Wood also enjoyed the supreme statements of cinematic auteurship made by the director Orson Welles. Wood's films embraced the accoutrements of genre (for example: melodrama in **Glen Or Glenda**, or the hybrid of science fiction and horror in **Plan 9 From Outer Space**) yet simultaneously aspired to (and, in the eyes of his fans, achieved) the aesthetic singularity of Welles' **Citizen Kane** (1941). Producing his movies outside of the confines of the studio system, Wood never achieved either fame or financial success for these films.

As a scriptwriter, Wood's credits included A.C. Stevens' **Orgy Of The Dead** (1965) and **Fugitive Girls** (1974), and Ed De Priest's **One Million AC/DC** (1969). During his later years Wood also subsidized his film-making practices by writing numerous tawdry sleaze paperbacks – many of which are now considered classics of their genre – such as *Censorship, Sex And The Movies, Diary Of A Transvestite Hooker, It Takes One To Know One, Killer In Drag, Devil Girls, Watts... The Difference*, and *TV Lust*. Wood's status as an outsider was further marked by his transvestism (and especially his almost legendary fetish for angora), which also provided the central theme for his debut feature **Glen Or Glenda** (aka **I Changed My Sex** aka **I Led Two Lives**).

Wood barely made a living from his artistic endeavours, and he died in poverty at the age of 54 in 1978, in a small apartment on Yucca Street, within spitting distance from downtown Hollywood, shortly before his films began to be recognized as the product of a genuine visionary and cinematic outsider.

2.

The Los Angeles born and raised film-maker Tim Burton grew up surrounded by movies and film culture, including fan magazines such as *Famous Monsters Of Filmland*. Through his continual youthful engagement with cinema Burton became aware of the films of Ed Wood, and he "grew up loving **Plan 9**, which is a movie you see when you're a kid and it remains with you."[3] For Burton, Wood's films are not mere examples of the "worst" cinema as lazily articulated in the Medveds' book, instead they are:

"special. ...There's a certain consistency to them, and a certain kind of weird artistry. I mean, they are unlike any other thing. He didn't let technicalities like visible wires and bad sets distract him from his story-telling. There's a twisted form of integrity to that."[4]

Not only was Wood a figure with whom Burton was familiar, Burton's own aesthetic shared similar reference points within the zones of gothic horror, melodrama, and B-movies, as his *oeuvre* testifies with films such as **Pee-Wee's Big Adventure** (1985), **Beetlejuice** (1988), **Batman** (1989), **Edward Scissorhands** (1990), and – perhaps most telling of all – the fifties UFO invasion sci-fi homage **Mars Attacks** (1996) – based on classic bubble-gum cards – which owes as much to **Plan 9 From Outer Space** as to more recognized classics such as Byron Haskin's 1953 sci-fi epic **War Of The Worlds**.

Tim Burton was originally scheduled to be the producer for **Ed Wood**, however he became interested in directing the bio-pic having read the script by Scott Alexander and Larry Karaszewski, and seeing something of himself in the figure of Edward D. Wood. Wood and Bela Lugosi met by chance in Los Angeles, and the two men became close friends, with Wood casting the aging and unemployed actor in his movies. This friendship lasted until Lugosi's death in 1958. Similarly Burton befriended Vincent Price during the production of his short film **Vincent** (1982), and subsequently cast Price in the role of the Inventor in the Frankensteinian fairy tale **Edward Scissorhands**. The two remained close friends until Price's death in 1993:

"He [Wood] befriended him [Bela] at the end of his life, and without really knowing what that was like, I connected with it on the level that I did with Vincent Price, in terms of how I felt about him. Meeting Vincent had an incredible impact on me, the same impact Ed must have felt meeting and working with his idol."[5]

Further, as Burton observed, "People think it's funny that I did this movie. Because I've been so successful, why would I want to make a movie about somebody who's not successful? But the way I feel about that, and him and me, is that any of my movies could go either way, they really could, and so the line between success and failure is a very thin one."[6]

Indeed, despite the global success of **Batman** and his reputation as a director, Burton had difficulties guaranteeing total artistic control over **Ed Wood** with Columbia, and he eventually took the project to Disney who, recognizing Burton's talent, gave him the freedom he desired.

3.

Ed Wood – the film – focuses on Wood (Johnny Depp) during the major part of his film career (roughly covering the period from 1952–1958), following Wood's direction of **Glen Or Glenda**, through his friendship with Bela Lugosi (Martin Landau), and ending at the Los Angeles premier of **Plan 9 From Outer Space**. The film introduces Wood at the "peak" of his career, and through his important and close friendships with Lugosi, Bunny Breckinridge (Bill Murray, in an understated cameo), Tor Johnson (George "The Animal" Steele), Criswell (Jeffrey Jones), Vampira (Lisa Marie), his girlfriend Dolores Fuller (Sarah Jessica Parker), and his girlfriend Kathy O'Hara (who plans to marry Edward at the film's close, played by Patricia Arquette). Burton frames the diagesis between two rain-soaked premiers – the first an all-but-deserted opening for a theatrical piece written and directed by Wood, the last being the packed crowd at Pantages Theater, Hollywood Boulevard, watching **Plan 9 From Outer Space**. Burton uses simple credits at the film's close to describe the actual fate of the characters, but spares the audience the sight of Wood's eventual decline into alcoholism and early death, instead allowing the film to end on the same eternally optimistic note that informed Wood's own attitude and work.

Stylistically the film echoes the B-movies of the fifties, Burton using the chiaroscuro of black and white stock to punctuate the film with references to generic classics – thus, for example, when Lugosi telephones Wood late at night the blinds cast a shadow across the bed, echoing the *mise-en-scène* of archetypal film noir. Similarly Howard Shore's score evokes the mood of fifties' horror, science fiction, and exploitation movies.

Burton – aware that much of Edward Wood's life is unknown – builds on the available biographical information, and imagines a meeting between Wood and his hero, the other - more successful – auteur, Orson Welles. The scene is telling; Wood, in full drag, walks into a bar and orders a drink, when he sees Welles sitting in the corner. Wood approaches Welles – as both a fan and fellow director. As the two talk Orson offers Wood advice, not once flinching at the director's choice of angora, unlike almost everybody else within the diagesis. The two are linked by their visionary status – Wood's transvestism is no longer an issue – both are outsiders to the homogeneity of the studio system, both are fighting for their respective visions, Wood to complete his epic, **Plan 9 From Outer Space**, while Welles, in a clear reference to his film noir masterpiece **Touch Of Evil** (1958), bemoans the fact the studio are insisting he casts Charlton Heston. Ultimately, in Burton's film, it is Welles whose advice enables Wood to complete his film.

Burton also ends the film with the climatic Los Angeles premier of Wood's **Plan 9 From Outer Space**. Of course, Wood never had a **Plan 9**

From Outer Space premier in the city[7], and certainly not in a Hollywood theatre. But the ending reflects Wood's mood, his ambition, his hope and his optimism. As an individual, Wood battled against all-odds and refused to be put off by unenthusiastic responses to his films, as he states during the sequence depicting the premier "this is the one, this is the one I will be remembered for". The line is ironic, it was this film which led to a resurrection of interest in Wood, but the resurrection of interest was – in part[8] – because of the film's (supposed) status as "worst movie"[9].

In many ways Edward D. Wood is very similar to Burton's other protagonists, who are suspended eternally outside the mainstream world, from which they will always remain distant: the heartbroken ice sculptor Edward Scissorhands, the vigilante Batman (and his monstrous counterpart in the form of the murderous psychopathic criminal mastermind the Joker), the eternally child-like Pee-Wee Herman, and the crazed horror-comedic figure of the bio-exorcist Beetlejuice. Whilst Wood is an actual figure, throughout the film he is presented as being an outsider, separated from the world by his very aesthetic and philosophical stance, and by his transvestism, surrounded by actors and personalities from the outer fringes of Hollywood. Wood's outsider status is punctuated in the film via his frustrated girlfriend Dolores as she screams, immediately prior to walking out on their relationship: "You

people are insane! You're wasting your lives making shit! Nobody cares! These movies are terrible!"

Burton's movie utilized an eclectic cast. Whilst the lead roles were cast with the recognizable figures of Johnny Depp and Martin Landau, several members of the cast were – like Wood's loyal troupe – unknowns: prior to her role in Ed Wood the model Lisa Marie had only had small roles, whilst the wrestler George Steele had never acted before. Burton's strategy was to cast a mix of recognizable figures and unknowns, both as an homage to Wood's style of film-making, but also to allow the film to generate "its own kind of weird energy"[10]. Burton even cast one-time Wood regular Conrad Brooks in brief a cameo as a bartender. This eclectic combination led to what Depp described as the "most ensemble picture I've ever made"[11].

Johnny Depp already had appeared in the title role in Burton's **Edward Scissorhands**, and the director and actor had established a friendship and mutual respect. Depp had already established a career in film, and was increasingly specializing in portraying characters who were different to traditional mainstream heroes, having appeared not only in **Edward Scissorhands** but also in the title role of John Water's **Cry-Baby**. As Denise Di Novi – Burton's co-producer on the movie – recognized: "Johnny is an actor who takes risks and gives unusual characters the special treatment and dignity they deserve"[12]. Burton asked Depp to appear in the film over lunch

at the Formosa Cafe in Hollywood, and Depp agreed to appear in the movie within ten minutes: "To me, it almost doesn't matter what Tim wants to film – I'll do it, I'm there. Because I trust him implicitly – his vision, his taste, his sense of humour, his heart and his brain".[13]

For Burton, **Ed Wood** offered the chance for Depp to engage with a role in a more open fashion than he had in their previous collaboration. Whilst Burton perceived Edward Scissorhands as a symbolic figure, **Ed Wood** was an actual person; while Scissorhands was a figure that represented – for Burton – an interior figure, Wood was an outgoing figure. This difference between the two characters would allow Depp to respond differently to the material.

Unlike the subjects of most bio-pics, however, much of Edward Wood's life remains undocumented save for the testimony of friends and family, which, of course, contain numerous contradictions. There is very little film footage depicting Wood, save for the quasi-autobiographical **Glen Or Glenda**; thus Depp's preparation for the role was complicated by a lack of available research materials. Depp had to interpret Wood from what was available with the aim of portraying Wood's "spirit"[14].

In his portrayal of Edward D. Wood, Depp constructed a character who appears to have great depth and a unique personal history. Whilst it would be easy for an actor to turn Wood into an exaggerated quasi-camp comedy figure – certainly Wood's failures, his less-than-ordinary-friends, and his reputation would allow for such a (banal) reading – thankfully Depp resisted such simplistic strategies. For Depp the fascination with Wood lay in Wood's visionary outsider status. Depp invested his performance of Wood with a combination of enthusiasm and quizzical naïveté signified by an almost permanent grin and wide-eyed wonder. This wonder is best illustrated during the sequence when Wood watches in wonder at Lugosi's ability to gesticulate magically at the television set, "Gosh Bela, how do you do that?" Wood asks, to which Lugosi replies: "You must be double jointed. And you must be Hungarian". Finally Depp invests Wood with a sincere tenderness and compassion, best illustrated in the moving scene in which Wood gives Lugosi an extra speech for **Bride Of The Monster**. Depp's portrayal of Wood radiates an energy for surviving a life against all odds.

Following the release of the film – and energized by the spirit of Edward Wood – Johnny Depp, Tim Burton, Martin Landau and Patricia Arquette wrote letters recommending that Wood should be given a star on Hollywood Boulevard alongside the greats.

NOTES

1. See Morton's absorbing essay on Ed Wood in Andrea Juno, V. Vale, eds, *Incredibly Strange Films*, Re/Search 10, Re/Search, San Francisco, 1986.

2. The image of Tor Johnson has become almost legendary, both as a best-selling Halloween mask, and also as a regular character in the comic strips of Drew Friedman. Johnson's other cult movie appearances include **The Black Sleep** (1956) and **The Beast Of Yucca Flats** (1961). Criswell, meanwhile, enjoys a small camp following, and a CD collection – *The Legendary Criswell Predicts!* - featuring some of the best of his wildly inaccurate prophesies is available via Mad Deadly Worldwide Communist Gangster Computer God, PO Box 420464, SF, CA 94142.

3. Tim Burton cited in Mark Salisbury, ed, *Burton on Burton*, Faber And Faber, London, 1995, p.130.

4. Tim Burton cited in Mark Salisbury, ed, *Burton on Burton*, p.130.

5. Tim Burton cited in Mark Salisbury, ed, *Burton on Burton*, p.131-134.

6. Tim Burton cited in Mark Salisbury, ed, *Burton on Burton*, p.131.

7. Although **Plan 9 From Outer Space** *was* previewed – under the title **Grave Robbers From Outer Space** – at the Carlton Theater, Los Angeles, on March 15th, 1957.

8. Whilst the Medveds' gloating book promoted the idea of **Plan 9 From Outer Space** as a contender for worst movie, the film was already enjoying a cult following as early as 1961, when it would regularly screen on late night television. Numerous fans had already come to enjoy the film long before the publication of the Medveds' books. Note, also, that legend has it that prior to broadcast, Wood would telephone friends, reminding them to tune in and watch.

9. Fans of **Plan 9 From Outer Space** – and Edward Wood's work in general – are divided, whilst some enjoy the film because of its supposed status as "worst film", others enjoy the film because it engages with a completely individual and utterly unique aesthetic and interpretation of the cinematic medium.

10. Tim Burton cited in Mark Salisbury, ed, *Burton on Burton*, p.139.

11. Johnny Depp quoted in Brian J. Robb, *Johnny Depp: A Modern Rebel*, Plexus, London, 1996, p.127.

12. Denise Di Novi quoted in Brian J. Robb, *Johnny Depp: A Modern Rebel*, Plexus, London, 1996, p.122.

13. Johnny Depp, Forward to Mark Salisbury, ed, *Burton on Burton*, 1995, p.xii.

14. Johnny Depp quoted in Brian J. Robb, *Johnny Depp: A Modern Rebel*, Plexus, London, 1996, p.123.

STRAIGHT TIME:
JOHNNY DEPP IN 'NICK OF TIME'

Nick Of Time was neither a critical nor commercial success on its initial release. This political conspiracy thriller opened in the US on the anniversary of the JFK assassination, "in a stroke of dubious taste", according to one critic, and received lukewarm, at best, reviews from others. Although the film was headlined by an A-list star, the public failed to show up at the box office in anything like the numbers they did for the Keanu Reeves vehicle, **Speed**. **Nick Of Time** has been compared with that film by a number of critics for providing Depp with a "straight" (i.e. commercial) role. Consequently, **Nick Of Time** received a limited theatrical release in the UK, where most viewers had to make do with catching the film on video or cable. Of all of Depp's films, **Nick Of Time** is among his least appreciated; even the minor cameo appearances in early films such as **A Nightmare On Elm Street** and **Platoon**, as well as *21 Jump Street*, the television series the actor was so unhappy with, have garnered Depp more attention.

Of course, **Elm Street**, **Platoon** and *21 Jump Street* were commercial successes, which exposed Depp's attractive features and bad boy/lost boy persona to large numbers of the public. In fact, although Depp has by now appeared in almost 20 films, many of which have been critical and/or commercial successes, the star's off-screen "private" life – specifically, his love life and run-ins with the law – continues to command as much attention as his on-screen appearances. Even though Depp's star and sex symbol status was confirmed by the time **Nick Of Time** was released in 1995, relatively few people saw the film and so it, and Depp's performance, remain under-appreciated.

There are a number of reasons that can be attributed to **Nick Of Time**'s critical and commercial failure; partly they concern Depp, and partly they are to do with audience expectations of the film's genre. **Nick Of Time**'s central gimmick has the proceedings unfold almost completely in real time, i.e. one screen minute equals one audience minute. While providing an unusual twist, the gimmick is also cumbersome and slows down the action by the need to dwell on unimportant details, by Hollywood standards. A ride in an elevator, for example, consumes five plus minutes of screen time. By the 1990s, Hollywood's perceived necessity for ever more speedy storytelling has seen plot exposition condensed into the opening pre-credit or credit sequences of films. In comparison to these kinds of formula films, **Nick Of Time** is slow-paced. This is a problem for an audience dieting on dumbed-down, speeded-up "popcorn movies" which fulfil, now more than ever before, that old cliché, the "roller coaster ride".

From a critical point of view, **Nick Of Time** fairs badly in terms of plot credibility. The elaborate assassination, for example, stretches believability. Watertight plotting is of paramount importance in the thriller genre; once it begins to leak, confidence in the film is lost. There is no love interest in **Nick Of Time** and romance, especially with an attractive lead like Depp, is a prime ingredient for commercial success. Characterisation also suffers from the real time scenario, which leaves little or no room for either background or development of the various characters. While it might be argued that characterisation in many Hollywood formula films is secondary to action, lifestyle details – fast cars, luxury homes, circles of friends, extended families – are selling points. **Nick Of Time** dispenses with these details for good reason – this is a film concerned solely with the moment, albeit 80 minutes' worth of them – but in doing so suffers in comparison with more formulaic Hollywood thrillers. Finally, **Nick Of Time** has a downbeat and rather abrupt ending. There is no reconciliation with a loved one, no final twist, no villain coming back from the dead, just a brief final shoot-out between the main players followed by a cut to an escaping villain.

Nick Of Time's failure might also be attributed to Depp, or more specifically the casting choice of Depp. Casting Depp as mild-mannered accountant Gene Watson has been seen as an example of mis-casting. One critic argued: "Depp as an average bespectacled accountant is about as well-cast as Charles Bronson was as a pacifist architect in **Death Wish**." Other critics have taken a slightly different standpoint, viewing the casting of Depp in an action film as an attempted "image overhaul" and a "bid for the mainstream". These critics have also made comparisons with Keanu Reeves' reinvention as an action hero in **Speed**, which lead that actor to a chain reaction of blockbuster roles. The fact that Depp has not followed **Nick Of Time** with more action hero roles is something those same critics have interpreted as a failed bid for the big time.

However, these critical reactions to Depp's performance amount to little more than the typecasting of an actor, while the public reception of **Nick Of Time** is explainable, in part, by audience expectations of a popular film genre, engineered by an industry that churns out formula movies. In short, the film and the star have fallen foul of assumptions and expectations. I want to argue that **Nick Of Time** breaks with the Hollywood formula for an action film such as **Speed**, that it is, in fact, another type of film altogether. I also want to argue that the role and the performance are not as dissimilar to other Depp characterisations as they at first appear to be.

First, a synopsis of the film: Union Station, Los Angeles. Single parent and accountant Gene Watson and his six-year-old daughter, Lynn, get off the train at noon and are accosted by Mr Smith and Ms Jones, who pose as

police officers. In a van outside the station, Smith (Christopher Walken) gives Watson a gun and threatens to kill Lynn if he doesn't go to the nearby Westin Bonaventure Hotel and murder a certain person by 1.30PM. Watson leaves for the hotel, shadowed by Smith, who is in radio contact with Jones who remains in the van to guard Lynn. The target turns out to be California Governor Eleanor Grant, who aroused the anger of conservative parties by reneging on campaign promises to big businesses. Watson attempts to alert the governor's security staff but finds they are in on the conspiracy. At gunpoint he makes her aid, Krista Brooks, take him to the governor's husband and campaign manager, Brendan Grant. However, Brendan is also in on the conspiracy, along with the Mystery Man, a business tycoon, and Smith, who is on the security team, murders Brooks. Shortly after 1PM, Watson convinces a shoeshine man named Huey to help him and, with the assistance of a number of hotel employees, sneaks into the governor's quarters and warns her of the plot. She doesn't believe Watson until her husband insists she attend her last speech of the day where her would-be assassin has told her she is to be shot. At the final speech, Watson shoots wildly to cause a panic, during which Smith fires on the governor but hits her bodyguard. Watson follows Smith outside to the van, where Huey has stopped Jones from killing Lynn. Smith is about to murder Lynn himself when Watson shoots him. In the aftermath, television news crews pick up the story of the conspiracy and the Mystery Man makes his escape.

At first glance, **Nick Of Time** does appear to be a straightforward action film. Director John Badham has a string of mainstream action movies to his credit including **Blue Thunder, Stakeout, Bird On A Wire, The Hard Way** and **Drop Zone**. Given Badham's career trajectory as a director for hire, it would be reasonable to expect another moderately successful, if uninventive action film. However, while the basic elements for success are in place – director, star, story, marketable concept (the real-time gimmick) – **Nick Of Time** digresses from the familiar formula in numerous ways.

A number of the digressions are to be found in **Nick Of Time**'s plotting details. Principally, the lack of love interest, Watson's killing of Smith and the final shot of the villain escaping, all break with the Hollywood norm. The lack of love interest prevents the casting of an attractive female co-star, denies the film sexual tension and makes obsolete the "reconciliation" or "reunion" closing shot, inherent to the Hollywood formula (cf. the genre's recent apotheosis, **Die Hard**). **Nick Of Time** also breaks one of the moral codes of conduct for Hollywood by having its lead character commit cold-blooded murder. Regardless of the level of provocation, the action hero kills only in self-defence and in the penultimate scene in **Nick Of Time**, Watson executes Smith. The final scene, in which the Mystery Man makes his escape in a limousine, is notable not only for the villain's escape, but also for being the very last shot of the film, also breaking with the formula, which requires the star to be present in the final scene.

The film's unusually subversive plot pits men against women, ethnicity against WASP and working class against the financial elite. The assassination is engineered by a group of powerful white men, the victim is a woman, the victim's sole trustworthy member of staff is a woman and aid ultimately comes from individuals working in the service industry, the three most significant of which are African and Native American in origin.

The most obvious digression from the Hollywood formula is the real-time gimmick (concept in Hollywood terminology). The concept in **Speed** was fast movement, and so the action was located, first aboard a plummeting elevator, then a bus on the freeway and, finally, on a runaway subway train. The concept in **Nick Of Time** is confinement and so the action is restrained. The action is confined, not just within a short time frame, but also within an enclosed space – the hotel. There is, after all, only so far an individual can move within 80 minutes. The scope of the action itself is thus limited. In this film's elevator sequence, for example, Smith wills Watson to kill the governor, but Watson resists and so no action occurs. In fact, the film's only major stunt sequence, in which Smith throws Watson off the hotel's balcony to drop 70 stories to his death, is revealed to be a dream. In **Nick Of Time** action is replaced with tension. With less spectacle on display and more suspense

underpinning the film, **Nick Of Time** has more in common with a thriller such as Alfred Hitchcock's **North By Northwest** than modern Hollywood action films.

By the time Depp took the role of Gene Watson he had already played a singing biker in **Cry-Baby**, a fairytale creature in **Edward Scissorhands**, a moody loner in **Arizona Dream**, a man-child in **Benny And Joon**, a transvestite B-movie director in **Ed Wood**, an existential Wild West wanderer in **Dead Man** and a Latin lover with mental health problems in **Don Juan DeMarco**. Since **Nick Of Time**, Depp has played a Native American martyr in **The Brave**, an undercover cop in **Donnie Brasco** and the drug-abusing Hunter S. Thompson in **Fear And Loathing In Las Vegas**. Compared to these parts, the character of Gene Watson is straight-laced. In point of fact, Watson is a straight-laced character by *any* standards. This is accentuated by the fact that there isn't much room given over towards characterisation in **Nick Of Time**. The few, simplistic details we are given suggest Watson is the most average of Joes. We learn that he is an accountant, a father and single parent. His dress code is conservative: a grey suit, tie, glasses, watch and wedding ring. Watson's status as a "normal" person is set up in direct opposition to the extraordinary situation he finds himself in, which heightens the drama; were Watson less "normal", the dramatic impact would certainly be reduced.

Watson is part of a long tradition of everyman characters, of which Cary Grant probably gives the most notable performance as the advertising executive in Alfred Hitchcock's **North By Northwest**. In fact, Hitchcock thoroughly explored and exploited the character type, casting Henry Fonda and Robert Donat in **The Wrong Man** and **The 39 Steps**, respectively. Hitch filmed everywomen, too: Joan Fontaine in **Rebecca**, Janet Leigh in **Psycho**. As a result an everyman character is now inevitably labelled as a "Hitchcockian hero", which was the case with Watson when **Nick Of Time** was released.

The everyman has a number of recognisable character traits. Firstly, he is, essentially, a victim of circumstance. To this end, it is of prime importance that the everyman be a passive character. Secondly, when the everyman takes action it is "out of character" by his own standards. The strength to do this often originates from an impulse to protect loved ones. Hence, the everyman is likely to have strong paternal, maternal and/or brotherly instincts. Thirdly, the everyman is trapped within a very constrictive set of circumstances – the traditional web of intrigue, labyrinthine plot, political conspiracy, etc. Gene Watson, **Nick Of Time**'s everyman meets all these requirements. He is both passive and naïve, which traits become evident when Watson first allows him and his daughter to be abducted by Smith and

Jones and then needs to be constantly goaded into action by Smith. As a single parent, Watson performs both the paternal and maternal functions for his daughter. Forced to commit an unthinkable crime, with no idea whom to trust and shadowed by Smith throughout the film, Watson is trapped within the public spaces of the hotel and within the diminishing time frame.

What is interesting about Depp's choice to play Watson is that the very characteristics that define the Hitchcockian everyman are exactly the attributes Depp has brought to his other more outlandish roles. Depp has played a number of characters, which combine passivity with naïvety. In the same year that **Nick Of Time** was released, Depp played another pen-pusher getting off another train in a very different film, **Dead Man**. Depp's clerk, William Blake leaves the civilised east and undertakes what is, essentially, a spiritual journey through the Wild West. Blake begins his travels as a blank book in which various oddball characters make their mark. In **Arizona Dream**, Depp plays another lost boy, Axel Blackmar, who is persuaded to attend his uncle's wedding in the Midwest, where he becomes involved in the love lives of a mother and her daughter. **Edward Scissorhands** saw Depp playing a variation on Frankenstein's monster, a freak creation who submits to the changeable will of a suburban community.

A second recurring trait in Depp's characters, paternity/maternity, informs his character in **What's Eating Gilbert Grape?**. Depp's title character is forced to play both father and mother as well as big brother to a fatherless Midwest family. A year later, Depp took the role of **Ed Wood**, the talentless transvestite movie director with boundless enthusiasm for his work. While directing various Z-grade productions, Wood assembles a cast and crew of misfits who become his adopted family. Wood strikes up a father/son relationship with one of the characters, the ageing Bela Lugosi.

Constriction, both metaphorical and literal, is also a recurring character trait in a number of Depp's roles. It's quite literally the case in **Edward Scissorhands**, where his creation is held together with a black leather bondage costume complete with buckles and straps from neck to ankles. In **Donnie Brasco**, Depp's undercover cop is caught between two worlds: his job and family life and the lives of the gangsters he first infiltrates and then is seduced by.

Depp's characters are loners, often with either a great weight of responsibility or an oppressive load to deal with. In **The Brave**, Depp's angelically-named Raphael sacrifices himself for his family by agreeing to be killed in a snuff movie for money. In **Cry-Baby**, his biker and gang leader Wade Walker is locked up in the jailhouse by the conservative establishment. This weight provides the characters with an underlying intensity, which has become a trademark in Depp's performances. In **Nick Of Time**, it is most evident during Depp's on-screen sparring with Christopher Walken's villain.

At the heart of these scenes is the opposition between the two characters. Smith badgers and bullies, one moment playfully, the next deadly serious, the man he has completely within his thrall; Watson takes the abuse, desperately seeking an alternative solution to his predicament. In the elevator scene, for example, Smith focuses an intense stare on Watson, willing him to kill his target. Watson sweats nervously, looking as if he is about to implode with the strain of attempting to figure out a way out of the situation. The mounting tension between the two actors is palpable and it finds release on screen twice, finally, at the end when Watson shoots and kills Smith, but first and most spectacularly during the dream sequence in which Smith hurls Watson off the balcony of the hotel 70 stories up. As if to underline the intensity of the performance and certainly signifying his commitment to it, Depp performed the stunt jump himself.

In comparison with his other career choices, Gene Watson is clearly a straight role for Depp. However, opting for this straight role is not the career digression it at first seems. Watson bears, as we have seen, a number of similarities to other Depp characters – passivity, naïvety, paternal and maternal qualities, a sense of confinement – and Depp invests the part with his customary acting intensity. Choosing an action rather than character driven film is a departure for Depp, but then **Nick Of Time** breaks with the Hollywood formula for action filmmaking. The film finally represents neither an attempt to reinvent Depp's image, nor make a bid for mainstream success. Depp's choice of roles remains as oddball as ever and none of the films he has made since **Nick Of Time** have had mainstream appeal. On this evidence it's arguable whether, in fact, playing Gene Watson in **Nick Of Time**, Depp has done his straight time at all. As Smith observes of Watson at one point: "You're not just a regular guy, see. I know that."

STRANGER IN A STRANGE LAND: 'DEAD MAN'

Those dark inky eyes and high cheekbones aren't the result of make-up and plastic surgery: Johnny Depp has often alluded to the Native American blood in his family heritage. Perhaps this is one of the reasons why he was drawn to his directorial debut, **The Brave**, in which he stars as a half-Mexican, half-Native American who agrees to sacrifice himself in a snuff movie in order to save his wife and children from poverty. **The Brave** – panned by critics when unveiled at the 1997 Cannes Film Festival and still searching for a distributor on both sides of the Atlantic – wasn't Depp's first on-screen brush with "Indians" and the West. That came the year before in Jim Jarmusch's one-of-a-kind arthouse Western, **Dead Man**.

Dead Man is set in a brutal yet strangely poetic American landscape at the end of last century, whereas **The Brave** is very much a contemporary take on the country's ethnic and socio-economic problems. And yet Depp sees close connections between the two periods – the metaphor of the snuff movie as genocide – as he explained at **The Brave**'s Cannes press conference: "In parallel to what happened 100 years ago, there were very subtle tactics as opposed to just chopping people's heads off and cutting pregnant women open, which is what American soldiers did. They also infected blankets with disease and dispensed them to the indigenous people. So the idea of selling your life is relevant."

The subject matter of both films might well have stirred up something in Depp's genetic mix, but the real attraction of **Dead Man** – in which he plays a Cleveland accountant and not a Native American – was its director. "I did **Dead Man** so I could work with Jim Jarmusch," the actor admitted. "I trust Jim as a director and a friend and a genius." Jarmusch has been a much respected figure on the American independent cinema scene since his cool and stylish feature **Stranger Than Paradise** appeared in 1984. Since then, his output has provided one cult favourite after another – including **Down By Law** (1986), **Mystery Train** (1989), **Night On Earth** (1991) and **Year Of The Horse** (1997) – while never grabbing the attention of mainstream audiences or setting the box office alight. These are exactly the parameters that seem to allow Johnny Depp the creative freedom to do his best work.

Jarmusch neatly fits into a similar niche filled by other filmmakers Depp admires. He, John Waters, Terry Gilliam and Tim Burton are as much outsiders (to the Hollywood league) as the characters they have created for Depp. In **Dead Man**, Depp is very much a stranger in a strange land, a meek accountant mistakenly uprooted from the civilised East and thrust into the

lawless West. But unlike Ed Wood in an angora sweater or Edward Scissorhands as a gothic mannequin in suburban USA, Depp's character in **Dead Man** gradually becomes at one with and conqueror of his immediate surroundings.

On a train bound from Cleveland to the remote town of Machine, a nervous Bill Blake (Johnny Depp) observes his fellow passengers between snoozes. At first they seem like respectable ladies and gentlemen; later in the journey, they're more like farmer folk; as he closes in on his destination, the compartment becomes full of unwashed frontiersmen in furs. The train's smokey-faced fireman (Crispin Glover) sits with him for a while. Blake says he has used the last of his money, following the funeral of his parents, to travel west and begin work as an accountant in the Dickenson Metalworks in Machine. During a strained conversation, the fireman wonders why Blake has come "all the way out here to Hell". The frontiersmen jump up and start shooting out of the windows at buffalo, while Blake cowers at the noise of the gunfire.

The train arrives at the end of the line in Machine, and Blake makes his way past coffin-makers, animal carcasses and prostitutes to the Metalworks. In the office, he is told that the position is already filled and is greeted with hostility and mocking laughter when he insists on seeing Mr

Dickinson himself. In Dickinson's inner office, the tyrannical boss (Robert Mitchum) points a double-barrelled shotgun at Blake and sends him away.

Blake wanders the muddy night-time streets of Machine and buys a bottle of cheap whiskey from a saloon. He watches as a young woman selling paper flowers, Thel Russell (Mili Avital), is thrown to the ground by a drunk. After helping her up, he walks her home; they flirt and go to bed. Thel's ex-lover Charlie (Gabriel Byrne) arrives unexpectedly in an attempt to make up with her. He shoots Thel as she moves in front of Blake; Blake takes Thel's pistol from beneath the pillow and, after firing wildly, fatally wounds Charlie in the neck. However, the bullet that killed Thel has lodged in Blake's chest. He gathers his clothes, escapes through the window, steals a horse and rides out of town. When he regains consciousness the following morning, he finds an Indian (Gary Farmer) trying to dig the bullet from next to his heart, but it is embedded too deeply.

Dickinson hires three bounty hunters – Cole Wilson (Lance Henriksen), Conway Twill (Michael Wincott) and Johnny "The Kid" Pickett (Eugene Byrd) – to bring Blake back, dead or alive, revealing that Charlie was his son. The Indian continues to care for Blake while on the move, with the bounty hunters on their trail. When he discovers his charge's name is William Blake, he confuses him with the famous poet-painter, believing that he truly is in the presence of a dead man. Blake himself now begins to question whether he is alive or dead. Like a vigilante training a pupil, the Indian praises Blake for killing a white man, saying that violence will now replace poetry as his means of expression. He then tells his own life story: captured by white men as a child, he was exhibited as a savage and transported to England where he was sent to school. On his return, however, his mixed blood and white man's education isolated him from his tribe. He is called "He who talks loud, says nothing", but prefers the name Nobody.

Nobody and Blake come upon a camp where Big George (Billy Bob Thornton), Benmont Tench (Jared Harris) and transvestite Sally Jenko (Iggy Pop) are cooking possum and beans. Blake approaches them and the trio pick over his clothes like vultures. They begin a strangely comic fight over Blake: Tench shoots Big George in the foot, Nobody cuts Big George's throat, Blake shoots Tench, and Nobody shoots Sally by accident.

Blake spots a wanted poster that puts a price on his head. Elsewhere the bounty hunters have also seen the posters and are annoyed that Dickinson, who hired them on an exclusive basis, has gone back on his word. Wilson kills Pickett for talking back to him. After eating peyote, Nobody sees Blake as a skeleton and paints Indian markings on the white man's face. Blake is growing weaker through hunger and blood loss, but Nobody abandons him, taking his spectacles. Two marshalls appear and, asking if they know his poetry, Blake kills one, whose rifle accidentally goes off, hitting the

other; Blake calmly finishes off the wounded man. The two remaining bounty hunters find the bodies and Wilson viciously crushes the head of one underneath his boot. Soon he also shoots the talkative Twill, cooks him up and eats him.

Blake, perhaps hallucinating, sees Indians in the forest and, next day, discovers a white man shot through by arrows. He then sees a fawn, shot in the neck, and after mingling their blood, lies down beside it. When he re-encounters Nobody, who is having sex with an Indian girl in a woodland clearing, he smiles for the only time since arriving in the west. Nobody promises to take him to "the bridge made of waters" where "many will be taken up to the next level of the world".

At a trading post, Nobody tells how the white man has callously destroyed his race by selling them infected blankets. Wanted posters displayed there raise the price on Blake's head to $2,000. The missionary shopkeeper (Alfred Molina) is in awe of Blake's celebrity, but is outwardly racist to Nobody. Blake, when asked for an autograph, stabs the man through the hand with a pen, then shoots him. Outside, Blake is shot in the arm, but kills his assailant with amazing accuracy. Nobody and Blake get into a canoe just before Wilson arrives at the trading post and follows them down the river. They arrive at an Indian camp where Blake drifts in and out of consciousness.

When he awakes, he is beside the sea, dressed in furs. Nobody prepares the canoe for its final journey and pushes Blake away from the shore. As he drifts away, Blake watches as Nobody and Wilson shoot each other.

Dead Man split the crowds when it premiered at the 1995 Cannes Film Festival. At that time, it was 134 minutes long and contained material – subsequently cut from the 120-minute version released in British cinemas – that caused the Australian Film Censorship Board to ban the film outright on account of its sexual violence, the first English language movie to receive such treatment since **Henry: Portrait Of A Serial Killer**. Most of the cuts, however, were made to tighten up what is, in its essence, an episodic journey that's driven by the clash between character and environment rather than some snappy plot. The deliberate pacing still irritates many viewers, but it gives the film a necessary sense of mysticism, using moments when the screen completely fades to black like the stanza breaks of an epic poem.

Following on from his portmanteau film **Night On Earth** and marking his first period piece, Jim Jarmusch settled on the Western as the initial point for **Dead Man**'s departure from traditional genre formats into a more loosely defined spiritual odyssey. The final result is a melting pot of influences: part buddy road movie (with horses and woodland trails taking the place of fast cars and lost highways), part chase movie, part fantasy quest with a knight attaining some Grail-like prize after undergoing various trials. Jarmusch, however, has his own reading of the material. "It is as though [Blake] passes through the surface of a mirror, and emerges into a previously unknown world that exists on the other side," he explains. "For Bill Blake, the journey of **Dead Man** represents life. For Nobody, the journey is a continuing ceremony whose purpose is to deliver Blake back to the spirit level of the world."

No major actor of his generation other than Johnny Depp could bring with him to the screen such an appropriate air of otherworldliness. His casting is a vital factor in allowing Jarmusch to achieve his aims. Depp's obvious physical beauty is a counterpoint to Machine's industrial ugliness; his smooth skin is unravaged by the West, unlike the lines, as deep as the Grand Canyon, on the faces of Lance Henriksen and Iggy Pop. "He's moody and very emotional and very sensitive," Jarmusch told *Harper's Bazaar* in December 1995. "In real life, sometimes it's hard for him to decide where to eat or what to do, but as an actor, he's very precise." That precision is very

important, for it is the technical basis that allows Depp to become the quiet centre of the movie, underlining how much his character is at odds with the physical and moral wilderness around him. What he brings to the film is the other side of the coin from Ed Wood's manic energy: his stillness, his delicacy, his skill at conveying vulnerability.

Depp's outward appearance in a film can hint at the often unspoken interior worlds his characters inhabit. In **Benny And Joon**, he paid direct homage to Charlie Chaplin, dexterously clowning around like the man-child the character is on an emotional level. In **Dead Man**, his look is much closer to Buster Keaton. Blake's loudly checked suit, spectacles and cravat tie – coupled with the way he clutches his bag and his silent, almost mournful expression – make him a naively clownish figure of fun from the opening scene onwards. Once again, his outsider status is made painfully apparent. Later in the film, when he is more at one with the mood of the frontier, he loses his glasses and covers himself up in furs.

However, this transformation from innocent abroad into outlaw in some men's eyes and famous poet in another's isn't simply a case of Blake unwittingly allowing the situation to remould him. As the Existentialists would argue, he makes his own decision to embrace his new-found twin destinies. "That gun will replace your tongue," says Nobody at one point. "You will learn to speak through it. And your poetry will be written in blood." Bill Blake kills men and so becomes at one with the West. As the film progresses, his clothing becomes less foppish and Depp makes the character tetchier – the mild-mannered accountant grows irritated by Nobody's "Indian malarky". When he loses his spectacles, he conversely becomes more accurate with a gun as Depp takes away Blake's look of fear to make him stronger and more determined: while it took three shots to nail Charlie, he barely needs to aim in order to kill his final victim outside the trading post. Even Blake's face must undergo change with zig-zag Indian markings. Only Johnny Depp, with his Native American blood, could make the transformation seem so complete.

Given the above definition of Blake's character and the narrative arc of the film, it's no surprise that premonitions of death appear even before the main titles, when the train's fireman warns Blake that, looking for a job out in the West, "you're just as likely to find your own grave". And when Blake's physical death is made inevitable because the bullet aimed at Thel becomes stuck next to his heart, another genre influence is added to Jarmusch's mix – the fatalist film noir, like **D.O.A.** or **Sunset Boulevard**, where in chronological narrative terms, the central character is dead, or as good as dead, before the first frame crosses the screen.

The Biblical/Christian notion that "in the midst of life we are in death" is central to the story and imagery of **Dead Man**. Like Clint Eastwood coming to town in a Sergio Leone spaghetti Western, one of the first sights to greet

Blake in Machine is a coffin-maker's workshop; but unlike The Man With No Name, he can't offer up a quip to indicate he'll win the impending showdown. The human skulls that lie in the streets beside animal carcasses find a parallel later in the film when Nobody's peyote-induced dream state projects a skull-like death mask onto Blake's face. Even the section of poetry by the "other" William Blake that Nobody quotes has a dark tone: "Every night and every morn/Some to misery are born/Every morn and every night/Some are born to sweet delight/Some are born to sweet delight/Some are born to endless night." It's clear that Bill Blake, as soon as he stepped on the train in Cleveland, was leaving behind any hope of sweet delight.

For the course of the film, Blake literally is the walking wounded; but even without the bullet that is slowly killing him, he's a marked man with a bounty on his head and a group of professional killers aching to pull the trigger. It seems appropriate that the "dead or alive" option handed out by Dickinson comes to mirror a similar idea introduced by Nobody and soon picked up by Blake himself: that this white man, sharing the name of a deceased poet and painter, is not among the living but is a dead man walking the Earth until he achieves a state of purification. Looked at in this light, **Dead Man** is very much a film about the process of preparing for and accepting the greatest mystery in life – death itself.

When, at the trading post, the dying missionary expires saying, "God damn your soul to the fires of Hell", Depp gives Blake's reply – "He already has" – a resigned nobility. However, it seems unlikely, given the spiritual progression of the film, that Blake is about to burn for eternity down below. If we read the film as a journey through Purgatory (or its non-Christian equivalent), then Blake is able to achieve final peace when he crosses the waters in his funeral canoe. The murders he has committed have, under the guidance of Nobody, purged the white man's impurities from him.

Jarmusch attempts to pull off these big philosophical ideas in the nominal form of a Western, making some distinctive and idiosyncratic artistic choices. First of all, he shot the film in black and white, calling upon the talents of Wim Wenders' regular cinematographer, Robby Muller. Then, instead of using period music or the wide orchestral sweeps that distinguish the modern Hollywood Western, he set Neil Young the task of writing the score. Jarmusch and Young had previously collaborated on the video for the latter's song "Big Time" and they'd later team up on the tour documentary feature film **Year Of The Horse**. Here, however, Young eschews his patented country rock style for a recurrent theme played on heavily distorted electric guitar – described by Sight And Sound as "Ennio Morricone wearing steel gloves". Young uses his instrument to create jagged flashes of noise and occasionally something akin to the rumble of thunder, but principally he sticks to an endlessly repeated theme that reflects the violence of story and remains at odds with beautiful landscape. The same tune becomes more melodic and gentle when played on acoustic guitar over the final credits, when Blake's peace has been attained.

At all times, Jarmusch sets up a contradiction between the violence of his subject and the artistic manner in which it is realised. Contradictory figures and moods are woven through the film, nowhere more so than the gallery of grotesques that provide cameo roles for an array of character actors. As Dickinson, Robert Mitchum sports a mane of grey hair to make him the lion king of this jungle frontier; but how truly imposing can a man be if he shares his inner thoughts with a stuffed grizzly bear? Later we see Iggy Pop in a dress and bonnet, telling the story of Goldilocks beside the campfire, and note that vicious bounty hunter Conway Twill can't sleep without his teddy bear. These touches establish a mood of surreal comedy that unsettles the viewer, particularly when a children's toy and a fairy tale can accentuate **Dead Man**'s clash between innocence and savagery. Again, the stumbling figure of Bill Blake and poster-boy looks of Johnny Depp provide the opposition to the cruel surroundings.

Death occurs in the film in many forms: as a necessity in self-defence, as callous villainy, as the job of a professional, as revenge on a lover or a race. Jarmusch further unsettles his audience by adding a touch of humour to numerous accidental shootings, which could be seen as a by-product of the Tarantino-led independent cinema of the mid-'90s. When Nobody examines a rifle and kills Sally the transvestite, it's hard not to think of **Pulp Fiction** and the demise of Marvin in the back of the car when Vincent Vega's trigger finger is nudged by a bump in the road. Jarmusch does not, however, glorifying gunplay as gangster chic. Any suggestion that the director believes there is beauty in death is literally crushed in the scene where bounty hunter Wilson puts his boot through the skull of the marshall killed by Blake. The almost tender image of a corpse lying with its head in the extinguished camp fire is, as Wilson says, "like a goddam religious icon" – and that is an image that cannot be allowed to exist in this unforgiving world. Bill Blake, with the physical appearance of Johnny Depp, is also too beautiful for the world in which he finds himself, and so his death is assured.

Jarmusch reckons the carnage he puts on screen "isn't exploitation or poetic Peckinpah slow-motion or isn't-it-cool-to-shoot-people; it has consequences. The film tries to show the ease with which you can adapt to violence, particularly in America. It's almost as if it becomes Johnny's job, something he does in order to survive as far as his own death. Johnny's subtlety and his physical presence enabled him to capture this essentially reactive side of his character, and he seemed to understand the emotional curve of the story without overdoing it."

Depp does indeed play a peculiar brand of outlaw in the film, but even as a soldier in **Platoon** or an undercover cop in **Donnie Brasco**, he's never a threatening tough guy. Perhaps there's the possibility that the off-screen Depp – the one who allegedly trashes hotel rooms, tattoos his hands and gets into fights with paparazzi photographers – would actually have been perfectly at home in the rough and tumble world of the Old West.

"He's treated like some movie star, but really he's an artist," is Jim Jarmusch's final assessment of Johnny Depp. Likewise Depp does not count himself in the same category as other pretty-boy actors. In the past he has turned down **Speed, Interview With The Vampire** and **Legends Of The Fall**, thereby deliberately setting himself apart from the likes of Keanu Reeves, Tom Cruise and Brad Pitt.

"He takes off-centre, artsy roles as an actor, and he's that way in his personality too," reckons Floyd Red Crow Westerman, who appears as Depp's father in **The Brave**. Depp did try his hand once at a commercial Hollywood thriller – **Nick Of Time** – and it clearly backfired for him; in Britain it was released straight to video. **Dead Man**, on the other hand, is a film set firmly in the history and geography of America, but it never feels like a product of the American film industry. Nor do **Fear And Loathing In Las Vegas** or **Edward Scissorhands**. Even a Johnny Depp mob movie like **Donnie Brasco** is directed by an Englishman, Mike Newell, and not the American master of the genre, Martin Scorsese.

Given this, it's worth noting that Depp is now actively cultivating a French connection: father of a young daughter by chanteuse and actress Vanessa Paradis, he also co-owns the Man Ray restaurant in Paris (with Sean Penn and Simply Red's Mick Hucknall) and in 1999 won an Honorary Cesar Award, the hugely prestigious French equivalent of an Oscar. Depp, the youngest-ever winner of the award, now joins the ranks of Orson Welles, Steven Spielberg and Sean Connery. The French clearly admire the unique qualities brought by Depp to **Dead Man** and his other screen work. It's as if he has, for all his Native American blood, carved himself as European a career as can be possible within American cinema.

COSA NOSTRA IMPOSTER: JOHNNY DEPP/DONNIE BRASCO

Mike Newell's **Donnie Brasco** takes its title from the alias chosen by undercover FBI agent Joseph Pistone, who infiltrated a New York Mafia family for over six years in the 1970s. Pistone spent the twelve years between 1982 and 1994 testifying against the various gangsters with whom he developed certain dubious bonds, leading to over 200 indictments and over 100 convictions. Pistone currently lives under yet a third identity under the FBI protection program, since the mob still has a long-standing $500,000 price on his head.

Donnie Brasco was released in 1997, to generally enthusiastic reviews. Critics regarded the film as bringing a fresh perspective to the gangster genre, reinventing the familiar tale of the undercover cop who gets in too deep as "an unadorned human tragedy, stripped of glamour and leavened with humour"[1]. Hailed as "the best mob film since **Goodfellas**"[2], the movie also won praise for its presentation of the mid-level Brooklyn hoods, and their ambiguous network of relationships ("there's something about the camaraderie, the subculture, the constant threat of violence, and the cadence of the dialogue..."[3]). Most of the reviews gave special attention to Al Pacino's brash performance as aging hit man Lefty Ruggiero, "a hateful man who inspires pity, even sympathy"[4]. **Donnie Brasco** was also widely considered to be Johnny Depp's first "mainstream" role, his potential escape from the "strange guy" niche, his "rite of passage" movie, enabling him to shed the burden of his pretty-boy teen-idol looks with a grounded, dirty, adult performance. As Mike Newell points out, Donnie Brasco is "a hard man, a brutal man... it's the strong, manly role that Hollywood wanted [Johnny Depp] to do for so long"[5]. "For Johnny Depp", writes Roger Ebert, "**Donnie Brasco** breaks new ground; he seems a little older here, a little wearier, and he makes the transition from stoolie to friend one subtle step at a time"[6].

The casting of Johnny Depp in the role of Brasco/Pistone is both significant and appropriate, and for a wide variety of reasons. Like Brasco/Pistone, Depp is a watchful, secretive actor with an apparent taste for danger, duplicity and disguise. He also seems to be a pathological role-player – somebody who comes into sharp focus and attains full life only when he loses himself in a role. Director John Badham, who cast Depp in his thriller **Nick Of Time**, describes him as "one of those identi-kit police drawings"[7], a shadow waiting to be given life by his next role. Newell calls him an "unploughed field", a man unencumbered by ego, and increasingly confident of his gift for transforming himself into anything he wants to be"[8]. And this is exactly how Pistone describes his undercover role as a Mafia imposter:

"Not every agent can work undercover. You have to have a strong personality. Strong means disciplined, controlled, confident. It doesn't mean loud or abrasive or conspicuous. It means your personality can withstand the extraordinary challenges and temptations that routinely go with the work... You have to be an individualist who doesn't mind working alone. Really alone, more alone than being by yourself."[9]

In preparation for his role as **Donnie Brasco**, Depp spent some weeks hanging out with FBI agent Joe Pistone. "I didn't think I would like him at first," recalls Depp. "I mean, you read his book and it sounds like it was written by a machine" (a very accurate description, as a matter of fact). "I thought he would be this gung-ho cop, this cold, uptight kind of guy, but Joe's a very neat person. We became friends."[10] Pistone, in return, was amazed at Depp's capacity for imitation. "He captured me 100% – my mannerisms, my walk, my talk," claims Pistone, who witnessed Depp absorb his personal characteristics right down to a nervous cough. "He absorbs so much... he doesn't try. It just comes to him. And he remembers everything. He's like a sponge."[11] Perhaps more than anything else, this convincing versatility – the ability to make himself into such a wide range of different personalities in each of his movie roles – qualifies Depp to play the role of Pistone's undercover operative.

The tense dynamic of the narrative of **Donnie Brasco** comes from Depp/Pistone's gradual immersion into the Bonnano Family, and the increasing ambivalence of his various loyalties. As the pressure mounts for him to become involved in Mafia violence, he needs to cut off his relationship with his worried wife (Anne Heche) and angry children. In the movie, Depp always seems much more at home hanging out on the street with the wiseguys than he does with his family, or in business meetings with his colleagues in the FBI. At one point, his wife comments on how similar he seems to be growing to the criminals he is pursuing. "I'm not becoming like them," he shouts, desperately. "I am them." In fact, Lefty and Donnie are more alike than not. Just as Lefty is little more than a cog in a futile machinery of justice and loyalty ("I'm a spoke on a wheel," says Lefty, "and so are you"), Donnie is treated with more compassion and understanding by the wiseguys on the streets than the FBI bureaucrats for whom he is risking his life and soul.

In effect – as Depp's muscular, laconic performance makes clear – Pistone likes being Donnie Brasco; he certainly prefers hanging out with a bunch of Mafiosos to working as an office-bound fed. Eventually we see him wanting to be "upped" in the Bonnano family as much for better infiltration as for personal gain ("I was so close to getting made and becoming a real

wiseguy that I could taste it," writes Pistone in his book). Finally, "Donnie Brasco" has infiltrated so far into the Mafia that he lives in daily fear of being both discovered by the Mafia as an agent, and being shot by the police for being a mobster (the FBI has a large file on the wiseguy "Donnie Brasco", unaware of his undercover status). Moreover, as Pistone explains, the physical closeness of the Mafia makes it virtually impossible for him to ever wear a wire:

"You develop feelings for people, even in this job... Some of these people develop feelings for you too... It was difficult to hide anything. I was in solid with these guys, and there was always the traditional hugging and kissing of cheeks. There was horseplay, wrestling around."

The most poignant element in the movie is the bond that develops between the innocent-looking, open-faced Depp and Al Pacino's very weary, unsuccessful and seedy low-ranking mob hitman Lefty Ruggiero. Lefty badly needs someone to trust – his son is a junkie, he suffers from "cancer of the dick", and his mob career is heading nowhere. Depp plays his scenes with Lefty as an awkward, lonely kid, allowing Lefty to take on the father-mentor role he so desperately needs to play. It soon becomes obvious that Lefty has

limitations that will prevent his promotion, and Donnie's big-chested strength and cocky street-smarts can compensate for Lefty's own failings. Instructing the sleazy, toothpick-chewing Depp in the rules and customs of the Mafia hierarchy, Lefty announces "I represent you; no-one can touch you now". In truth, however, he needs Donnie as much as Donnie needs him – perhaps even more.

Many of Lefty's peculiar traits and qualities are taken from Pistone's account of his character, such as his taste for white wine spritzers, his talent for cooking, his chain-smoking of English Ovals and his refusal to wind down his car windows or ever turn on the air conditioning ("you wanna kill me with that draft?"). Pistone also vividly describes the way Lefty sits around his pokey flat in a track suit watching nature documentaries on television ("[h]e had a big colour TV and a VCR," writes Pistone, "and a cable connection into which he had tapped illegally, like all the wiseguys, so it was for free"). Perennially discontent, Lefty's combination of petty childishness and high dignity make him appear at times something of a tragic figure, sometimes hurt and lonely, often alienated and pathetic. The unusual friendship than develops between Lefty and Donnie is also something Pistone describes in his account:

"With Lefty, it was twenty-four hours a day. I stayed in hotel rooms with him, changed clothes in the rooms, stripped to swimming trunks to go sit around the pool... 'Donnie,' Lefty says, 'do me one favour. I love you. I'd rather do five years than lose your friendship. Do everything right over here because you can name your own ticket, believe me.'"

As Donnie rises in the Bonnano family, it becomes increasingly clear to him that when the time arrives for him to come out, Lefty will be in the position of having vouched for a traitor. This heightened sense of anxiety is betrayed by Depp's increasingly awkward posture and strung-out body movements, sustaining the tension in the relationship to such an extent that the loyalty between the two men provokes a crisis which easily overshadows the murderous lies and schemes of the world in which they are inextricably caught.

The first way in which Lefty helps Donnie weasel his way into the Bonnanos' favour is to change his appearance. When he first starts hanging out with the wiseguys, Depp sports a black leather jacket, slicked back black hair, the obligatory gold jewellery, and a sleazy moustache. Lefty – himself, it must be added, no model of sartorial *savoir faire* – soon has Depp wearing '70s suits with wide lapels, very flamboyant, loose Hawaiian shirts, sports jackets and oversized sunglasses. He also makes Donnie shave off his moustache – another detail taken straight from Pistone's account of events:

"Lefty was fastidious. He told me to shave off my mustache and cut my hair. 'No real wiseguys wear mustaches,' he said, 'except some of the old mustache Petes. You gotta look neat, dress right, which means at night you throw on a sports jacket and slacks.'"

Depp starts his performance as Brasco/Pistone as a dumb-faced, smirking, awkward, gum-chewing kid, who is gradually coached by Lefty in the ways of the Bonnanos, and soon develops a more confident, slightly shifty, aggressive, capo-style persona. Little details of being "in the family" that Depp picks up from Pacino include never to carry his money in his pocket (wiseguys always use a roll), never to pay for his own drinks, and the all-important distinction between "a friend of mine" and "a friend of ours". In one of the most memorable scenes in the movie, a highly strung-out Depp lies on a sofa with his eyes tightly shut, rubbing a cold can of beer over his forehead, explaining to his FBI supervisors the many different implications of the favourite wiseguy phrase, "forget about it".

This conversation, however, is an improvisation, an example of screenwriter Paul Attanasio's use of dramatic license with Pistone's story.

Certainly, Pistone learned a great deal from Ruggiero – he recounts at length how he learned to adjust his demeanour by watching Lefty, how to ask the right questions, how to see the right things, how to act and think like a wiseguy. But in Pistone's account of the case, much of the advice Lefty gives him is somewhat less quirky and charming than the movie makes it out to be. At one point in the book, for example, Pistone recalls a piece of advice Lefty gives him about women:

"'[T]hat's a thing about wiseguys. You go out and kill somebody, but don't swear in front of a female. And if a female swears, she's a putana, a whore. If Louise said "fuck", I'd throw her out the window'."

As he spends more and more time hanging around with the wiseguys, Depp's sleazy, sinewy, wide-eyed Brasco gradually becomes increasingly familiar with the grubby pathos of the Bonnanos' world. Donnie's initiation into the Mafia typifies the film's unpretentious vision of mobster life – its stupidity, its violence, its lack of dignity. The world Donnie Brasco is introduced to is a world of lonely men who cluster around seedy "social clubs", sharing out cheap stolen goods and the proceeds of broken parking meters, desperately striving to feed the demands of their bosses. Much of the time Donnie spends with the Bonnanos involves nothing more glamorous and exciting than hanging around bars and coffee shops, playing cards and complaining that business is bad. The wiseguys also tend to indulge in silly, Tarantino-style conversations about – for example – the superiority of a Lincoln over a Cadillac.

This is another element of **Donnie Brasco** that critics found so refreshing – the impression it conveys that we are seeing a more realistic depiction of the mob than that portrayed in most romanticized Mafia films. One reviewer described the cast of wiseguys as "loud, crude and vicious... Even the crimes they are typically shown to be involved with are, for the most part, penny ante in nature. The only really shocking criminal acts that are shown are the violence they commit on one another"[12].

However dull and tedious this routine may seem, however, it is distinctly glamorous compared to the long days Pistone describes, which he spends sitting around playing backgammon and listening to wiseguys boast and bullshit to one another. The holes in Lefty's underwear, for example, provide a standing joke amongst the capos that seems to last the entire six years Pistone spends undercover. "Unlike the images we get in movies like **The Godfather**, the Mafia in real-life is repetitious," claims Pistone. "Conversations are mind-numbing. 'What are we gonna steal today? How are we gonna steal it?'" Ironically, Pistone also recalls a scene in a restaurant when a strolling guitarist wanders past the wiseguys' table, and they wistfully ask him to play them the theme from **The Godfather** ("the guy sang it in Italian, and then in English").

Depp's mean, laconic, driven Donnie Brasco shares a number of significant characteristics with Pistone's alter ego. We see Depp doing push-ups in the gym, for example, working on his biceps, still wearing all his gold jewellery. Similarly, Pistone claims that to ease the tension of his situation, he used to try to run every day, and lift weights at the health club in his apartment building ("I didn't know any wiseguys at the time who were doing that," he adds. "It was okay, I was just considered a health nut"). Also – quite remarkably, given his circumstances – Pistone doesn't drink alcohol, has never tried drugs, and allegedly remains faithful to his wife, despite six years of sexual invitations from numerous Mafia groupies.

And yet, as Pistone remarks, his long stretches spent away from home in the role of Donnie Brasco start to bother his family more and more. His wife, Maggie, grows angry and distant ("what kind of a marriage is it," his wife would say over the phone, "when the husband is never home?"). In the scenes with his wife, the macho, defensive Depp appears sullen and sulky, tense and petulant, striding around irritably, trying to assert his authority over a family who scarcely know him any more. In the scenes with his children, he makes an uncomfortable father. At one point in his account, Pistone claims that "if we hadn't had so strong a marriage, it probably wouldn't have survived these years," but there's a sense of denial here, and perhaps a note of protesting too much.

And yet, despite these similarities with Pistone's account, the film version of **Donnie Brasco** condenses and simplifies his six years undercover, reducing some characters into composites, and omitting many of the complexities of the case. Some of the most dramatic scenes in the film are actually fictional extrapolations, including the near exposure of Donnie's wire when the manager of a Japanese restaurant orders him to take off his shoes. Another fictional scene is Donnie's airport meeting with an old friend, whom Depp, starting to enjoy his status as a wiseguy, is forced to smack in the face to prevent his cover from being blown.

The film also omits references to other FBI agents who were also working undercover with Pistone from time to time, though we do follow him to his regular coffee shop meetings with his FBI boss, when Depp invariably appears a little more fraught and pensive than usual. The film is also set almost exclusively in Brooklyn and Florida, whereas Pistone explains how his Mafia business also takes him to California and Milwaukee, and sometimes for substantial periods of time.

The film also simplifies and romanticizes Donnie's relationship with Lefty, emphasizing the older man's growing affection for Depp's macho but vulnerable young gangster. Pistone, however, explains how he grew increasingly frustrated with the real Lefty, who would embarrass him in public, call him a "fucking nitwit idiot" and basically treat him "like a piece of shit" ("[t]here were times I could have strangled him on the spot... with everything else there was to worry about, I had to take his daily shit... That's how fed up I was with Lefty").

Also simplified is the character of Sonny Black, played by Michael Madsen as another crazed psycho à la Mr. Blond in Tarantino's **Reservoir Dogs**. Even more reminiscent of **Reservoir Dogs** is the scene in prison, after the wiseguys get arrested for illegal gambling, with Madsen deliberating on who amongst them all is the rat ("[t]hat cocksucker Sonny Red," snarls Madsen, "he rubs my nose in slaughter, all because of some fucking rat"). As Sonny Black, Madsen constantly struts around in his cowboy boots, and comes out with lines like "I tell you now, we'd better start earnin', or somebody's gonna get clipped". In the film, Depp/Brasco lives in terror of Sonny Black, concealing his fear beneath a vacant, open-mouthed expression of feigned confusion. And yet in his account of the case, Pistone explains how, as he begins to grow increasingly irritated with Lefty, he grows closer and closer to Sonny Black, spending time at his home, helping him clean out the coops of his racing pigeons. Says Pistone:

"All the wiseguys could see how close I was to Sonny... I felt a kind of kinship with him... Sonny was good at what he did. He wasn't a phoney. He didn't throw his weight around. He was a stand-up guy. For reasons that are hard to explain, I liked him a lot."

The most poignant scenes in the movie come right at the end, when it becomes increasingly clear that the termination of Depp's project will involve a terrible betrayal of his mentor, Lefty. In one scene, Depp tries awkwardly to encourage Lefty to take money from him, buy a boat, and sail away with Louise, his wife. There is also a very strong suggestion that Lefty, learning of Donnie's betrayal, prefers to take his own life rather than subject himself to mob justice, leaving a final message for Donnie: "if it was going to be anyone, I was glad it was him".

In reality, the termination of Pistone's project led to a number of internal mob hits, though Lefty Ruggiero was not one of the victims. Mafia boss Tony Mirra – a character omitted from the movie – was discovered in a car in a Brooklyn parking lot in March 1982, shot four times in the head. In August 1982, the body of Sonny Black was found washed up in the Mariner's Harbor section of Staten Island, with its hands chopped off – an indication of a Mafia hit and a special signal that the victim had violated mob security. "I was sorry it was Sonny; I was glad it wasn't me," writes Pistone – an interesting twist on the words put in the mouth of Lefty in the movie.

The main effect of Pistone's project, however, was to cause significant leadership problems in the Mafia, resulting in the arrest of a number of top-level bosses, engendering a prevailing sense of mistrust and wariness in each family, and in relations across family lines. Also, at least according to Pistone, the Americanization of the Mafia has weakened the strong attachment to kinship and "family honour" that the older wiseguys used to have. As Pistone puts it, "La Cosa Nostra – 'Our Thing' – is becoming 'My Thing' in the hands of the younger generation". As for Pistone himself, the transition from wiseguy to regular citizen has not been an easy one. He still finds himself adopting a "wise guy attitude" with waiters and salesmen whom he judges to be inadequately respectful or compliant.

As for the real Lefty Ruggiero, he has steadfastly refused to co-operate with the government and join the Federal Witness Protection Program to reduce his sentence. A Mafia contract has been put out on him for his association with "Donnie Brasco", yet he still refuses to turn stoolie. Pistone expects Ruggiero to make an attempt on his life as soon as he's released on parole.

Interestingly enough, according to Pistone, word on the streets has it that all the wiseguys who read Pistone's book thoroughly enjoyed it – that is, with the exception of Lefty Ruggiero, who apparently read the book, and didn't enjoy it at all. Perhaps he was more favourably impressed with the film version. After all, having Al Pacino play you in a movie must be some kind of compensation for a fifteen-year stretch in the big house, however little. And yet it seems that, in the end, the real Lefty Ruggiero would prefer quite simply to "forget about it".

NOTES

1. Margaret McGurk, "Donnie Brasco Reinvents Mobster Film" (movie review), *The Cincinatti Enquirer*, 22nd November 1997.

2. Patrick Stoner, "Donnie Brasco", *Flicks*, 5th March 1997.

3. Ibid.

4. McGurk.

5. Mike Newell, cit in Roger Ebert, "Donnie Brasco" (review), *Chicago Sun-Times*, 22nd February 1997.

6. Ibid.

7. John Badham, cit in Richard Schickel, "Depp Charge", *Time*, March 3 1997.

8. Newell, cit in ibid.

9. All quotations taken from Pistone, Joseph, with Richard Woodley, *Donnie Brasco – My Undercover Life In The Mafia*, Signet: New York, 1989.

10. Depp, cit in Stoner.

11. Pistone, cit. in Schickel.

12. Richard Andrews, "Donnie Brasco" (review), *Indianapolis Herald*, 12th March 1997.

'FEAR AND LOATHING IN LAS VEGAS'

1.

"Hilarious comedy about a business trip which becomes more trip than business"[1]

Fear And Loathing In Las Vegas, in its guise as both book and film, continues to escape pigeonholing. I found a copy of the book in my local library in the Health section, hidden among books with names like *My Daddy Was A Junkie* and *How To Tell If Your Teenager Is Using Drugs*. Most bookshops stock all Hunter S. Thompson material in their fiction section, regardless of content, although I half-expected to find it in the travel section, lurking among Berlitz guides to Vegas to stun the unsuspecting browser. The company promoting the video release (see above quote), seem even more confused.

It's worth noting how the author views the book, and his own brand of "gonzo" journalism, which derives from William Faulkner's idea that the best fiction is far more true than any kind of journalism:

"My idea was to buy a fat notebook and record the whole thing, as it happened, then send in the notebook for publication – without editing... But this is a hard thing to do, and in the end I found myself imposing an essentially fictional framework on what began as a piece of straight/crazy journalism. As true Gonzo journalism, this doesn't work at all – and even if it did, I couldn't possibly admit it. Only a goddamn lunatic would write a thing like this and claim it was true."[2]

This kind of mixture of fact and fiction was to prove very popular in the '70s, but as far as the style goes, this one's probably closer in spirit to *The Naked Lunch* than *In Cold Blood* – Burroughs' contention that in most of his writing he is recording what he experiences – "I am a recording instrument... I do not presume to impose 'story' 'plot' 'continuity'"[3] – holds true here as well: there is some "story" imposed on the first third, but after then *Fear And Loathing...* is almost as fragmentary as a Burroughs book. As far as "faction" books about drug culture go, moreover, it's very much one from the inside looking out compared to the "Black shiny FBI shoes" take of Tom Wolfe in *The Electric Kool-Aid Acid Test*.

In terms of categories the central actors and the director of the film are equally difficult to pin down. Depp, who could so easily have become a

Brad Pitt-style pin-up, has consistently gone for difficult and often marginal roles, and nails Hunter S. Thompson perfectly – bald pate, drug mumble and twitchy mannerisms all over. He's barely recognisable as being the same actor who played Edward Scissorhands. Benicio del Toro is even more of a revelation, entirely unrecognisable from his previously svelte and louche days; here he sports a Hispanic Buddha belly, wild hair and the out-of-control demeanour of a grizzly on acid. Gilliam's films are also becoming more difficult to read, more ambiguous. Where once there was one central protagonist with whom the audience was clearly meant to identify in his films, there have in his past three releases been two – Jeff Bridges and Robin Williams in **The Fisher King**; Bruce Willis and Brad Pitt in **Twelve Monkeys**; and here Johnny Depp and Benicio del Toro. Audience alignment in terms of the ideas of the films has also become more murky; Gilliam's idealism seems to be increasingly tempered by a dark cynicism and a sense of terminal breakdown.

The film's video release promotes the film as a side-splitting comedy, using phrases like "brilliant and insane humour" and "one man's funniest time on earth" to persuade the Jim Carrey crowd to part with their cash – but it's certainly not a comedy; or not, at least, any more than **The Texas Chain Saw Massacre**. A look at the official website or interviews with those involved with the making of the film shows an altogether more radical and serious agenda at work:

"Fear And Loathing has all the elements of classic mythical stories. Raoul Duke and Dr Gonzo are the two anti-heroes that go to hell, take the magic cookie, tilt at windmills and survive, and we go through that journey with them."

(Laila Nabusi, producer)

The references implicit here – Dante, Cervantes and Carroll – are made explicit elsewhere on the site, as the set designer refers to his brief being "*Alice In Wonderland* meets Dante's *Inferno*", while Cassavetti, also involved in producing the film, refers to Duke and Dr Gonzo as "an early '70s, post-hippie version of Don Quixote and Sancho Panza." There seems here almost a determination to justify making the film of **Fear And Loathing** within a classical context, which is perhaps unsurprising considering that the film is, ostensibly, about two men using inordinate quantities of illicit narcotics, with none of the preachy moralising which normally accompanies Hollywood depictions of drug use. In a world in which the BBFC still refuses to grant a certificate to the loveable but dated **The Trip** (1967), and the drug hysteria of the '80s continues apace, one of the most amazing things about the film is that it was made at all. Steve Pulchaski ended his comprehensive essay on hallucinogens in cinema, first published in *Shock Xpress*, thus: "The 1980s government-backed drug-blitz put a veritable end to these films, and it'll be some time until full-scale, pharmaceutical-drenched productions like **The Trip** loom on the horizon."[4] As Jack Stevenson has pointed out in a piece on drugs in Hollywood cinema, though, it's hard to argue that the film glamorises drug use, with its nightmarish acid scenarios and endless scenes of Dr Gonzo doing the big spit:

"This... doesn't so much glamorise drug use as celebrate the squalour and chaos of the experience. That's a new one. While the subject matter (drugs, drugs and more drugs) would automatically incite conservative opposition, the approach of the film could only hopelessly confuse the issue. By any measure, a Hollywood film that contained so much moral ambiguity was something new."[5]

For the most part, the film sticks very closely to the book, although in the second half certain scenes are chosen from the inchoate and unfilmably fragmentary second half of the book while others are ignored. The very fact of actually seeing the antics of Raoul Duke and Dr Gonzo on screen highlights certain themes from the book which tend to be neglected by the casual reader in favour of the focus on narcotic excess. For a start, it hadn't really occurred to this reader before that the pair get up to some pretty loathsome activities regarding the people they meet: while the scene involving the hitchhiker at the beginning is merely amusing, scenes featuring Christina Ricci as a naïve Streisand fan given acid by Dr Gonzo, seen again later in the film looking broken and hopelessly lost after having been ditched by the duo (this latter scene, notably, is not taken from the book), and the attack on Ellen Barkin as a waitress towards the end, make the pair seem ugly and cruel. This is particularly true of the latter instance, which is played straight – no camera tricks, no filters or bizarre, cartoonish effects – for a jarring impact akin to seeing real footage of a cat killing a mouse cut into a *Tom & Jerry* cartoon. More important, though, is the idealistic subtext running through the film and book. **Fear And Loathing In Las Vegas** isn't just the demented ramblings of some substance-addled hack abusing a huge expense account. This is about a search for something far more important: the American Dream.

But what does that mean? The phrase is used pretty freely to denote a concept most would be familiar with, even if they can't explain it. Take your pick from the following: white picket fences; Mom's apple pie; strive and succeed; the pick'n'mix availability of mall culture; land of the free; independence; the pioneer spirit; a Coca-cola dispenser on every street corner in the world... It's such a nebulous and woolly concept that it can usually only be touched on peripherally – through the patina of age, in the endlessly

revised saga of the Wild West, or through a psychedelically-enhanced hippy take on the stars and stripes. The film and the book, both explicitly concerned with this search (the subtitle of the book is "A Savage Journey To The Heart Of The American Dream"), pit two apparently different approaches to the American Dream against each other, and it's worth considering the film within these two conflicting traditions, which can be seen to represent counterculture and establishment – as a psychedelics film, and as a gambling film, or more properly a film about Las Vegas.

2.

"We had two bags of grass, seventy-five pellets of mescaline, five sheets of high-powered blotter acid, a salt shaker about half full of cocaine, and a whole galaxy of multi-colored uppers, downers, screamers, laughers... and also a quart of tequila, a quart of rum, a case of Budweiser, a pint of raw ether and two dozen amyls."

This is not the place to go into a history of drugs, or even more specifically, psychedelics, in the cinema – both have been expertly covered before.[6] Although all kinds of drugs are used in the film, it's the psychedelics which remain to the fore. The CGI acid effects are bang-on and memorable, especially when compared to ludicrous attempts of the past to portray visuals on-screen; the pair give the impression of tripping almost perpetually, no matter what else they've taken, which is chemically realistic – acid tends to eclipse most other drugs when taken together; adrenochrome doesn't, as far as I know, exist, and can be viewed as a metaphorical "drug too far"; and looking at the IMDb "user's comments"[7], a lot of viewers rate **Fear And Loathing** as the most realistic depiction of acid use they've seen, this often being their principal comment.

The drug use in the film is however heavily contextualised. There are constant reminders that this is the aftermath of the hippy era – Vietnam footage is unsubtly playing on TVs throughout, with the use of the *Ride Of The Valkyries* theme early on recalling the helicopter attack from **Apocalypse Now**, and reference is made early on to the ugly end of the sixties – Manson, Altamont, Nixon etc. The film begins with stock footage of protests and hippies "freaking out", more of which is used later as Duke reminisces about the time when "we were riding the crest of a high and beautiful wave...", and the soundtrack places the pair firmly in "this foul year of our Lord, 1971".

As has been well documented, parts of the countercultural movement of the sixties identified heavily with an idealised view of America, some seeing themselves as following the spirit of the country's founding fathers. Drug use was seen as being in the pioneering spirit and also an issue of personal freedom – how could anybody legislate against an individual choosing to ingest a substance? The producer's sympathies are clear:

*"**Fear And Loathing** is finally about the American Spirit. We are adventurers and outlaws, forging new territory all the time in a free country. There's been a lot of clamping down on such creativity in recent years, and this movie offers an antidote to that state of mind... we have a tradition in this country of not being afraid to say whatever the truth is of that time or moment in spite of what's going on."*

Gilliam's take on all this is hardly subtle – in a mescaline trip before the journey begins Duke waves a tattered American flag back and forth as the pair lie in the surf; an American flag is used to snort ether from; an adrenochrome-riddled Duke wraps himself in the American flag to protect himself from a devilish Gonzo; and Hendrix's "Stars & Stripes" features on the soundtrack – not to mention Duke's rapid-fire mumblings to do with the "American Dream": "Horatio Alger gone mad on drugs in Las Vegas". Duke and Dr Gonzo, while surely part of some kind of counterculture, can hardly be considered as hippies, though – there's no love and peace here, with Gonzo's knife and Duke's Magnum taking centre stage a few times too

many, nor any desire for consciousness expansion. Their cynicism and "drugs for drugs' sake" angle is presented as what has helped them to survive where others have burnt out, even as their journey is in a way a desperate search for some kind of redemptive quality in American culture. Shouldn't have gone to Las Vegas, then...

One of the key passages in the book is quoted verbatim in the film:

"We're all wired into the survival trip now. No more of the speed that fuelled the sixties. That was the fatal flaw in Tim Leary's trip. He crashed around America selling consciousness expansion, without ever giving a thought for the grim meathook realities that were lying in wait for all those who took him seriously, all those pathetically eager acid freaks who thought they could buy peace and understanding for 3 bucks a hit. But their loss and failure is ours too. What Leary took down with him was the central illusion of a lifestyle that he helped create. A generation of permanent cripples, failed seekers who never understood the essential old mystic fallacy of the acid culture – a desperate assumption that somebody, or at least some force, is tending the light at the end of the tunnel."

It seems as though almost every major player in Hollywood has made a '60s revisionist film now, whether brutal Vietnam visit or dangerously naïve reworking in the **Forrest Gump** mould. Oliver Stone has made a career out of it, with **Natural Born Killers** in particular utilising a explicitly psychedelic sensibility in its approach. But Gilliam doesn't glorify psychedelics and their culture as Stone is prone to do – the visions of Duke and Dr Gonzo are ugly and uncomfortable, revealing less a vision of heaven than a spiky and hellish netherworld. There is hope and idealism in **Fear And Loathing**, but it's almost there by relief, something conspicuously absent from the atrociously vulgar Las Vegas of 1971, a nostalgic yearning for an energy, "a fantastic universal sense that whatever we were doing was right, that we were winning..."

3.

"Las Vegas is a city built on myths. Lies, really... None of the Vegas myths is bigger ... than the one that goes like this: 'it's possible to drift into town with only a few bucks and leave a week later with a fortune'. That's the elemental Vegas myth, the one that turns normally responsible men into fools and pensioners into paupers. Were it not for the gambling public's unwavering faith in the Big Myth, Las Vegas' casinos wouldn't win billions a year... gamblers harbor an inchoate fantastic hope that their meager plunge might lead to something big. They dream they might be the lucky soul who makes the Vegas myth come true. The fact is, it never happens."[8]

Only Hollywood outdoes Las Vegas in the USA's illusion-building stakes, and has long incorporated a perceived Vegas glamour into its mythos. It's only

recently, with films like **Casino**, that the crassly commercial side of Vegas has been the principal focus, beyond the glitz and sparkle, and **Fear And Loathing** plays at times like some demented twin of the former film – a peacenik de Niro and Pesci on ether.

The impeccably designed Las Vegas of **Fear And Loathing** – garish clothes, clashing patterns and impossible geometries that even a John Waters film wouldn't dare attempt – does bring to mind American icons, but less Horatio Alger than P.T. Barnum: out and out hucksterism with a side order of dwarfs rather than a "strive and succeed" mentality. The Bazooka circus is a phenomenal piece of work – "what the whole hep world would be doing on a Saturday night if the Nazis had won the war" – whose visitors almost all look more freakish than Duke and Dr Gonzo, and whose games are so weird they must exist somewhere: "Shoot The Vital Organs" (with darts resembling hypodermic needles); a toss game called "Knock The Kid's Teeth Out"; a shooting gallery featuring M16 rifles and moving ducks wearing conical Vietnamese farmers' hats; one game is even hosted by what appears to be a Klansman.

Duke only actually gambles once, and loses – "Learn to enjoy losing" – and this might indicate that the Las Vegas setting is almost incidental to the story. It isn't. Las Vegas represents a town built in the middle of the desert for no other reason than to make money, and, as in the Konik quote above, plays on a hope that can be considered as one facet of the American Dream. The Bazooka circus is, moreover, "the vortex... the main nerve", and proves so ugly that even Dr Gonzo can't handle it.

This approach to the American Dream would seem on the surface to be the polar opposite to the hippy ideal – there's no search for "truth" here, no appeal to any motivating factor less crass than greed. But the situation is more ambiguous than that:

"Vegas is so full of natural freaks – people who are genuinely twisted – that drugs aren't really a problem, except for cops and the scag syndicate. Psychedelics are almost irrelevant in a town where you can wander into a casino any time of the day or night and witness the crucifixion of a gorilla – on a flaming neon cross that suddenly turns into a pinwheel, spinning the beast around in wild circles above the crowded gambling action."

Every character or scene in the film, uncoloured by the pair's drug use, is as much a sideshow attraction or circus act as their actual hallucinatory experiences – and they're sometimes even more extreme. **Fear And Loathing** uses almost as many dwarfs as **Time Bandits**, and there's no yardstick of "normality" by which to judge Duke and Dr Gonzo – the lumpen grey DAs of the convention, fat-necked pitbulls one and all, are as freakish as any of the circus acts from the Bazooka. The "real" world of Las Vegas is so bizarre that the line between this and the drug-induced madness of Duke and Dr Gonzo is irreversibly smudged – Vegas has pre-empted their visions and made them into commercially viable spectacles. The principal theme in Gilliam's other films, of madness being the only way a sensitive soul can understand an absurd universe, is here in a way turned on its head – there's no "understanding" to be had here, but only a sense of disorienting absurdity. This takes us back to Duke's "light at the end of the tunnel" point above – looking for meaning and believing in higher purpose here can only end in disaster. Just enjoy the ride.

As Linda Ruth Williams has pointed out in a perceptive review of the film in *Sight & Sound*:

"The relationship between the establishment and its counterculture mutates into one of mutual dependence as the film progresses. 'Ether is the perfect drug for Las Vegas,' Duke intones as they enter Bazooka circus. 'In this town they love a drunk – fresh meat.'"[9]

Here we see the relationship between two ostensibly polarised factions becoming one less of ambiguity than of mutual reliance. This theme can be considered on a small as well as large scale: Duke and Gonzo are mutually reliant, with Duke like the classic straight man, constantly trying to keep Gonzo calm and curb his wilder excesses, which is ironic in itself considering traditional lawyer/client relations. Taking the theme still further, the characters of Dr Gonzo and Duke can even be considered as one person, with Gonzo appearing as a drug-induced apparition or projection whenever Duke gets high. The theory works well within the film, as a pattern emerges: Duke takes drugs and finds Dr Gonzo committing heinous and reprehensible acts – again and again. Dr Gonzo doesn't appear when Duke is straight, and even tempts him back to Las Vegas when he attempts to escape, to re-enact the first half of the film on an even grander scale.

4.

*"My guess is that today's audience wants this film desperately. I think they need it. That's why I've been referring to **Fear And Loathing** as a cinematic enema for the '90s – just clean out the system."*

(Terry Gilliam)

Gilliam clearly had high hopes for this film, and for the impact it might make on what he sees as a stale time for cinema. The film didn't do very well when released, though, and is unlikely to be massively successful as a video rental.

It was generally panned by critics, who found it indulgent and pointless, and often didn't find favour with fans of the book, who found it confusing. The filmmakers and actors are to be saluted, however, for having the courage to indulge in such a bizarre and ambitious endeavour. Depp and del Toro, in particular, give among the best performances of their careers, respectively.

Roger Ebert, a fatuous but high-profile American critic, was unsurprisingly less than impressed by the film, and made the following comment about Depp's performance:

"As for Depp, what was he thinking when he made this movie? He was once in trouble for trashing a New York hotel room, just like the heroes of 'Fear

And Loathing In Las Vegas'. What was that? Research? After River Phoenix died of an overdose outside Depp's club, you wouldn't think Depp would see much humor in this story."[10]

Other journalists also drew parallels between work on the film and Depp's "wild child" reputation. Stories of all kinds of madness, principally involving narcotics, small arms and explosives, filtered out of Woody Creek, Colorado, while Depp stayed with Thompson to prepare for the part. Thompson is notoriously difficult to get along with – Alex Cox, first slated as director on the project, was taken off following personal differences with the writer, and by the time of the film's première Gilliam and Thompson had also fallen out.

No such problem for Johnny Depp, though – he and Thompson had been friends before the project got off the ground, and remained close through the shooting. Depp:

"I think one of the things that helped with the initial meeting between us was that we're both from Kentucky. Hunter is, beneath it all, a real Southern gentleman... I wanted to make Hunter proud, because his story deserved all the attention and all the focus. So I just tried to make myself look as much like him as possible. I shaved my head on top, and just left a kind of shorthaired chinchilla around the sides. Hunter's ears are larger than mine, so I wore small devices to make mine poke out a little more. And there's a unique body language that Hunter has, and I could feel myself clicking into it once we started."

It seems likely that Depp's sympathetic portrayal of Thompson will have endeared him still further to the writer. Seeing Depp in twitchy, balding and manic mode, once the viewer gets over the initial shock, is utterly convincing, nailing Thompson perfectly.

Depp's choice of films throughout his career has demonstrated that he is interested in taking risks, in working with directors who have an individual vision, such as Emir Kusturica and Jim Jarmusch – and although he's an eminently marketable commodity, he hasn't gone down the Hollywood pin-up route to solid commercial success. It's probable that he's been the key factor in having films like **Ed Wood** and even **Fear And Loathing** green-lighted by the studios, and for that he is owed a debt of gratitude, especially at a time in which Hollywood studios seem otherwise terrified of making films with a distinctive flavour.

I suspect finally that **Fear And Loathing** wasn't generally much liked because it wasn't what people expected – it's altogether too queasy and disorienting, with Depp about as far from a sex symbol as he's ever been, and it resists the temptation to give its message a saccharine coating. On its own terms, however, it's a true gonzo classic – just enjoy the ride.

NOTES

1. CIC video promotional material.

2. This, and all other unattributed quotations, are from the excellent official **Fear And Loathing** website, url: www.fear-and-loathing.com, or from the novel itself (*Fear And Loathing In Las Vegas*, Hunter S. Thompson, Paladin 1972). Virtually all of the dialogue and narration in the film is taken directly from the novel, and the quotations listed here are all part of the film's narration.

3. William Burroughs, *The Naked Lunch*, John Calder edition 1964, p.221. First published in English by Olympia Press, Paris 1959.

4. *Shock Xpress* vol 3, #1, Summer 1989, p.32. This piece was revised and updated for Critical Vision's collection of Pulchaski's writings, *Slimetime*, in 1996, but the comment quoted here stands.

5. *Blimp Film Magazine* #39, p.58. This curious Austrian magazine, with articles in English and German, is well worth seeking out, not least for Stevenson's excellent piece.

6. See 4 and 5 above.

7. This refers to the Internet Movie Database, on which "users" can post comments.

8. *The Man With The $100,000 Breasts* – Michael Konik (Huntington Press, USA, 1999).

9. *Sight & Sound* November 1998.

10. *Chicago Sun-Times* on-line review: www.suntimes.com/ebert/ebert_reviews.

A JOHNNY DEPP FILMOGRAPHY

A Nightmare On Elm Street (1984)
Private Resort (1985)
Platoon (1986)
Slow Burn (1986) (TV)
21 Jump Street (TV series, 1987/90)
Edward Scissorhands (1990)
Cry-Baby (1990)
Freddy's Dead: The Final Nightmare (1991, uncredited)
What's Eating Gilbert Grape (1993)
Benny & Joon (1993)
Arizona Dream (1993)
Ed Wood (1994)
Nick Of Time (1995)
Don Juan DeMarco (1995)
Dead Man (1995)
Cannes Man (1996)
Donnie Brasco (1997)
The Brave (+ director, 1997)
Fear And Loathing In Las Vegas (1998)
L.A. Without A Map (1998)
Sleepy Hollow (1999)
The Ninth Gate (1999)
The Astronaut's Wife (1999)
Just To Be Together (1999)

INDEX OF FILMS

Page number in bold indicates an illustration

DENNIS HOPPER *Jack Hunter (editor)*
MOVIE TOP TEN

DENNIS HOPPER One of the most talented but controversial actors of recent decades, almost as notorious for his off-screen hell-raising as he is for his roles in such powerful films as his self-directed **The Last Movie**, David Lynch's **Blue Velvet**, and Tim Hunter's **River's Edge**.

Jack Hunter (author of film studies *Inside Teradome* and *Eros In Hell*) has selected his own chronological Top Ten of Dennis Hopper's movies, which are analysed in illustrated, in-depth essays by some of the best cutting-edge film critics of today. The result is both an incisive overview of Dennis Hopper as an actor, and an anthology of films by some of the leading cult directors of recent decades such as Wim Wenders, Tobe Hooper, David Lynch, Tim Hunter, Henry Jaglom, Curtis Harrington, and Hopper himself.

Featured films include: **Night Tide, The Last Movie, Tracks, Speed, The American Friend, Out Of The Blue, Texas Chainsaw Massacre 2, Blue Velvet, Rivers Edge**, and **Paris Trout**.

DENNIS HOPPER
MOVIE TOP TEN

easy rider
blue velvet
the last movie
river's edge
out of the blue
paris trout
tracks
night tide
the american friend
texas chainsaw massacre 2

CINEMA   Trade paperback   1 871592 86 0   192 pages   169mm x 244mm   £12.95

HARVEY KEITEL *Jack Hunter (editor)*
MOVIE TOP TEN

HARVEY KEITEL One of the most versatile and acclaimed actors of recent years, always willing to take on new, challenging roles ranging from the dissolute cop in Abel Ferrara's Bad Lieutenant and trigger-happy robber in Tarantino's **Reservoir Dogs**, to the taciturn settler in Jane Campion's **The Piano**.

Jack Hunter (author of film studies *Inside Teradome* and *Eros In Hell*) has selected his own chronological Top Ten of Harvey Keitel's movies, which are analysed in illustrated, in-depth essays by some of the best cutting-edge film critics of today. The result is both an incisive overview of Harvey Keitel as an actor, and an anthology of films by some of the leading cult directors of recent years, including Quentin Tarantino, Martin Scorsese, Nic Roeg, Abel Ferrara, Spike Lee, James Toback, and Jane Campion.

Featured films include: **Fingers, Mean Streets, Cop Killer, Bad Timing, Bad Lieutenant, Dangerous Game, Reservoir Dogs, The Piano, From Dusk Til Dawn**, and **Clockers**.

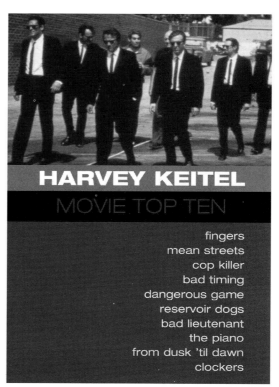

HARVEY KEITEL
MOVIE TOP TEN

fingers
mean streets
cop killer
bad timing
dangerous game
reservoir dogs
bad lieutenant
the piano
from dusk 'til dawn
clockers

CINEMA   Trade paperback   1 871592 87 9   192 pages   169mm x 244mm   £12.95

CREATION BOOKS

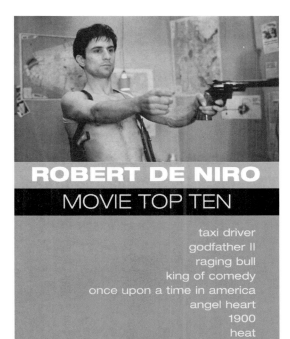

ROBERT DE NIRO
MOVIE TOP TEN

taxi driver
godfather II
raging bull
king of comedy
once upon a time in america
angel heart
1900
heat
cape fear
jackie brown

ROBERT DE NIRO *Jack Hunter (editor)*
MOVIE TOP TEN

ROBERT DE NIRO. One of the most versatile and acclaimed actors of recent years, famous for the uncompromising method approach he brings to roles ranging from the psychotic Travis Bickle in Martin Scorsese's seminal **Taxi Driver**, to the nerveless robber of Michael Mann's **Heat** and the loser in Tarantino's **Jackie Brown**.

Series editor Jack Hunter has selected his own chronological Top Ten of Robert De Niro's movies, which are analysed in illustrated, in-depth essays by some of the best cutting-edge film critics of today.

The result is both an incisive overview of Robert De Niro as an actor, and an anthology of films by some of the leading directors of recent decades such as Martin Scorsese, Michael Mann, Quentin Tarantino, Sergio Leone, Bernardo Bertolucci, and Francis Ford Coppola.

Featured films include: **Taxi Driver, Raging Bull, Angel Heart, Once Upon a Time In America, Jackie Brown, King of Comedy, Heat, 1900, Cape Fear, and Godfather II.**

CINEMA   Trade paperback   1 871592 88 7   192 pages   169mm x 244mm   £12.95

JOHNNY DEPP
MOVIE TOP TEN

donnie brasco
edward scissorhands
fear and loathing in las vegas
what's eating gilbert grape
nightmare on elm street
platoon
nick of time
ed wood
cry-baby
dead man

JOHNNY DEPP *Jack Hunter (editor)*
MOVIE TOP TEN

JOHNNY DEPP. One of the most enigmatic and uncompromising actors of recent years, famous for a wide variety of movies ranging from Tim Burton's gothic fable **Edward Scissorhands** and lurid pulp movie tribute **Ed Wood**, to Terry Gilliam's psychedelic, paranoiac drug epic **Fear And Loathing**.

Series editor Jack Hunter has selected his own chronological Top Ten of Johnny Depp's movies, which are analysed in illustrated, in-depth essays by some of the best cutting-edge film critics of today. The result is both an incisive overview of Johnny Depp as an actor, and an anthology of films by some of the leading cult directors of recent decades such as Tim Burton, Jim Jarmusch, Terry Gilliam, John Waters, and Wes Craven.

Featured films include: **Edward Scissorhands, Donnie Brasco, Ed Wood, Cry-Baby, Fear And Loathing In Las Vegas, What's Eating Gilbert Grape, Nightmare On Elm Street, Platoon, Nick Of Time, and Dead Man.**

CINEMA   Trade paperback   1 871592 89 5   192 pages   169mm x 244mm   £12.95

CREATION BOOKS

① KILLING FOR CULTURE

Kerekes & Slater

Killing For Culture is a definitive investigation into the urban myth of the "snuff movie". Includes: FEATURE FILM – from *Peeping Tom* to *Videodrome* and beyond; MONDO FILM – from *Mondo Cane* to present day 'shockumentaries'; DEATH FILM – from *Faces Of Death* to real deaths captured on film such as live-TV suicides, executions, and news footage.

Illustrated by stunning photographs from cinema, documentary and real life, **Killing For Culture** is a necessary book which examines and questions the human obsession with images of violence, dismemberment and death, and the way our society is coping with an increased profusion of these disturbing yet compelling images from all quarters. Includes filmography and index.

"Well-researched and highly readable, Killing For Culture *is a must-have."*
– FILM THREAT

CINEMA/CULTURE   Trade Paperback   1 871592 20 8   169 x 244mm   288 pages   £14.95

② INSIDE TERADOME

Jack Hunter

Freakshows – human anomalies presented for spectacle – have flourished throughout recorded history. The birth of the movies provided a further outlet for these displays, which in turn led to a peculiar strain of bizarre cinema: Freak Film. **Inside Teradome** is a comprehensive, fully illustrated guide to the roots and development of this fascinating, often disturbing cinematic genre.

Including: Teratology: freaks in myth and medicine; the history of freakshows, origins of cinema; influence of sideshows on cinema; use of human anomalies in cinema; freaks and geeks; bizarre cinema: mutilation and other fetishes; illustrated filmography; index; over 350 photographs. From the real-life grotesqueries of Tod Browning's *Freaks*, to the modern nightmare vision of *Santa Sangre*, **Inside Teradome** reveals a twisted thread of voyeuristic sickness running both through cinema and the society it mirrors.

CINEMA/CULTURE   Trade Paperback   1 871592 41 0   169 x 244mm   256 pages   £14.95

③ DEATHTRIPPING

Jack Sargeant

Deathtripping is an illustrated history, account and critique of the "Cinema Of Transgression", providing a long-overdue and comprehensive documentation of this essential modern sub-cultural movement. Including: A brief history of underground/trash cinema: seminal influences including Andy Warhol, Jack Smith, George and Mike Kuchar, John Waters. Interviews with key film-makers, including Richard Kern, Nick Zedd, Cassandra Stark, Beth B, Tommy Turner; plus associates such as Joe Coleman, Lydia Lunch, Lung Leg and David Wojnarowicz. Notes and essays on transgressive cinema, philosophy of transgression; manifestos, screenplays; film index and bibliography.

Heavily illustrated with rare and sometimes disturbing photographs, **Deathtripping** is a unique guide to a style of film-making whose impact and influence can no longer be ignored.

CINEMA/CULTURE   Trade Paperback   1 871592 29 1   169 x 244mm   256 pages   £14.95

④ FRAGMENTS OF FEAR

Andy Boot

Fragments Of Fear is an illustrated history of an often neglected film genre: the British Horror Movie. The book examines a wide range of British horror films, and the stories behind them, from the early melodramas of Tod Slaughter right through to Hammer and their rivals Tigon and Amicus, plus mavericks like Michael Reeves, sex/horror director Peter Walker and more recent talents such as Clive Barker, director of *Hellraiser*. Films discussed range in scope from the sadism of *Peeping Tom* to the mutant SF of *A Clockwork Orange* and the softcore porn/horror of Jose Larraz' *Vampyres*.

With plentiful illustrations, author Andy Boot unravels a tangled history and discovers many little-known gems amid the more familiar images of Hammer, including a wealth of exploitational cinema, to establish the British horror movie as a genre which can easily stand up to its more lauded American counterpart in the depth and diversity of its scope.

CINEMA   Trade Paperback   1 871592 35 6   169 x 244mm   288 pages   £14.95

CREATION BOOKS

⑤ DESPERATE VISIONS

Jack Stevenson

John Waters is the notorious director of *Pink Flamingos, Female Trouble, Desperate Living* and *Hairspray*, amongst other cult movie classics.

Desperate Visions features several in-depth interviews with Waters, as well as with members of his legendary entourage including Divine, Mary Vivian Pearce, Mink Stole and Miss Jean Hill. George & Mike Kuchar are the directors of such low-budget/underground classics as *Sins Of The Fleshapoids* and *Hold Me While I'm Naked*. Their visionary trash aesthetic was a great influence on the young John Waters.

Desperate Visions includes extensive interviews with the Kuchars, as well as a comprehensive assessment of their career and influence. Also included is a unique feature on actress Marion Eaton, star of the gothic porn epic *Thundercrack!*.

With many rare photographs, filmography and index, **Desperate Visions** is an essential introduction to the wild world of John Waters, and to the outrageous camp/underground film tradition which his movies exemplify.

CINEMA/CULTURE   Trade Paperback   1 871592 34 8   169 x 244mm   256 pages   £14.95

⑥ THE NAKED LENS

Jack Sargeant

The Naked Lens is a vital collection of essays and interviews focusing on the most significant interfaces between the Beat writers, Beat culture and cinema; films by, featuring, or inspired by: WILLIAM S BURROUGHS • ALLEN GINSBERG • JACK KEROUAC • CHARLES BUKOWSKI • BRION GYSIN ANTHONY BALCH • RON RICE JOHN CASSAVETES • ANDY WARHOL • BOB DYLAN • KLAUS MAECK • GUS VAN SANT *& many others*

Including interviews with writers such as Allen Ginsberg, directors such as Robert Frank and actors such as Taylor Mead; plus detailed examination of key Beat texts and cult classics such as *Pull My Daisy, Chappaqua, Towers Open Fire* and *The Flower Thief*; verité and performance films such as *Shadows, Don't Look Back* and *Wholly Communion*; B-movies such as *The Subterraneans, Beat Generation* and Roger Corman's *Bucket Of Blood*; and Hollywood-style adaptations from *Heart Beat* and *Barfly* through to Cronenberg's *Naked Lunch*.

CINEMA/BEAT CULTURE Trade Paperback 1 871592 67 4   169 x 244mm   288 pages   £12.95

⑦ HOUSE OF HORROR

Jack Hunter

HAMMER FILMS remains one of the most successful and legendary of all British film companies. Their name is synonymous with gothic horror throughout the world.

House Of Horror traces the complete history of Hammer, from its early origins through to its golden era of classic horror movies, and presents a comprehensive overview of Hammer's importance and influence in world cinema.

House Of Horror includes interviews with Hammer stars Christopher Lee and Peter Cushing, detailed analysis of all Hammer's horror and fantasy films and their key directors, and dozens of rare and exciting photographs and posters; plus a fully illustrated A–Z of key Hammer personnel from both sides of the camera, a directory of unfilmed projects, a complete filmography, and full film index.

Third, expanded edition

CINEMA   Trade Paperback   1 871592 19 4   169 x 244mm   224 pages   £12.95

⑧ MEAT IS MURDER!

Mikita Brottman

Violent death, murder, mutilation, eating and defaecation, ritualism, bodily extremes; cannibalism combines these crucial themes to represent one of the most symbolically charged narratives in the human psychic repertoire.

As a grotesque figure of power, threat, and atavistic appetites, the cannibal has played a formidable role in the tales told by members of all cultures – whether oral, written, or filmic – and embodies the ultimate extent of transgressive behaviour to which human beings can be driven.

Meat Is Murder! is a unique and explicit exploration of the stories that are told about cannibals, from classical myth to contemporary film and fiction, and features an in-depth illustrated critique of cannibalism as portrayed in the cinema, from mondo and exploitation horror movies and arthouse classics. It also details the atrocious crimes of real life cannibals of the modern age, such as Albert Fish, Ed Gein, Jeffrey Dahmer and Andrei Chikatilo.

CINEMA/CULTURE   Trade Paperback   1 871592 90 9   169 x 244mm   208 pages   £14.95

9 EROS IN HELL

Jack Hunter

SEX: The history of "pink" movies, from *Daydream* to *Ai No Corrida* and beyond, including the pop avant-garde violence of Koji Wakamatsu films such as *Violated Angels* and *Violent Virgin*. Bondage and S/M from *Moju* to *Captured For Sex* and Kinbiken rope torture.
BLOOD: From *Shogun Assassin* and *Psycho Junkie* to the killing orgies of *Guinea Pig* and*Atrocity*; from the "pink horror" nightmare *Entrails Of A Virgin* to the post-punk yakuza bloodbaths of Kei Fujiwara's *Organ* and Takashi Miike's *Fudoh*.
MADNESS: Homicidal psychosis, hallucination, mutation: *Tetsuo*, *Death Powder*, the films of Shozin Fukui such as *Pinocchio 964* and *Rubber's Lover*. Post-punk excess, nihilism,violence, suicide: *Labyrinth Of Dreams*, *Squareworld*, *Tokyo Crash*.
    Eros In Hell examines all these movies and many more besides, is profusely illustrated with rare and unusual photographs, comprising a unique guide to the most prolific, fascinating and controversial underground/alternative cinema in the world.

CINEMA   Trade paperback   1 871592 93 3   169 x 244 mm   256 pages   £14.95

10 CHARLIE'S FAMILY

Jim VanBebber

Charles Manson and The Family. The Love and Terror Cult. The Dune Buggy Attack Battalion. Devil's Witches, Devil's Hole. Jim Van Bebber's mind-blowing movie **Charlie's Family** is the most accurate and uncompromising cinematic portrayal of the exterminating angels of Death Valley '69, a psychotic assault of sex, drugs and violence that propels the viewer headlong into the Manson experience.
    Charlie's Family reconstructs the cataclysms of creepy-crawl and the Tate/La Bianca murders in vivid relief, showing us not only a devastating acid blood orgy but also the ways in which one man's messianic power held sway over an entire killer korps of sexually submissive yet homicidal believers.
    The illustrated screenplay of **Charlie's Family** contains nearly 100 amazing photographs, including 16 in full colour, as well as the complete script and 16 original storyboards. It also includes the definitive illustrated essay on Manson-related movies, written by Jim Morton, main contributor to *Incredibly Strange Films*, as well as an introduction by esteemed underground film critic Jack Sargeant.

CINEMA/TRUE CRIME   Trade paperback   1 871592 94 1   169 x 244 mm   192 pages   £14.95

11 RENEGADE SISTERS

Bev Zalcock

From boarding school to women's prison, biker packs to urban vigilantes, rampaging girl gangs have long been a staple feature of exploitation/independent cinema.
    Renegade Sisters examines the whole history of girl gangs on film, focusing on B-classics like Russ Meyer's *Faster, Pussycat! Kill! Kill!*, Herschell Gordon Lewis' *She-Devils On Wheels*, and Jack Hill's *Switchblade Sisters*; Women-In-Prison movies such as Stephanie Rothman's *Terminal Island* and Jack Hill's *Big Doll House*, with Pam Grier; camp SF like *Cat Women Of The Moon* and *Queen Of Outer Space*; plus many other deviant displays of girl power from various genres, right through to Todd Morris and Deborah Twiss' ferocious, post-Tarantino *A Gun For Jennifer*.
    Renegade Sisters also looks at Queercore girls; the feminist/lesbian movies of Barbara Hammer, Jennifer Reeder, Anie Stanley and others, and includes interviews with film makers Vivienne Dick and Julie Jenkins, as well as *A Gun For Jennifer* writer/ producer Deborah Twiss. With dozens of photographic illustrations.

CINEMA/WOMEN'S STUDIES Trade paperback 1 871592 92 5 169 x 244 mm   208 pages £14.95

12 BABYLON BLUE

David Flint

Filmed erotica and adult entertainment has finally come of age. Porn has at last become something that can be increasingly freely and openly enjoyed, and celebrated as a specialist leisure activity in its own right, with its own history and critical lineage. Despite decades of resistance, the long-established hardcore porn production houses have built an alternative film industry, complete with its own visionaries, superstars and standard-bearers.
    Babylon Blue examines the '60s roots of global modern-day erotic cinema – from naturist films to the "nudie-cuties" of Russ Meyer – through to various incarnations of Euro-porn and hardcore, charting the rise, decline and resurrection of the genre since the early '70s. Finally, author David Flint expertly chronicles the so-called New Porn Generation – the New Wave of adult movies, as epitomised by the stylish and sophisticated films of Andrew Blake, Michael Ninn and the Dark Brothers.
    Visually loaded with profuse and daring illustrations, **Babylon Blue** is the last word on sex cinema, featuring profiles of key directors, producers and performers, and detailed critiques of the finest adult movies of all time.

CINEMA/CULTURE   Trade paperback   1 84068 002 4   256 pages   169 x 244mm   £16.95

⑬ HOLLYWOOD HEX *Mikita Brottman*

From the myths of old Hollywood to recent on-screen accidents, the motion picture industry has long been associated with violent and untimely death. Hollywood has always been a magnet for suicides, murders, mysterious accidents and brutal mayhem; the simple fact is that, in the age of motion pictures, human death has become an inescapable part of show business. **Hollywood Hex** is a study of films that have, in one way or another, resulted in death and destruction. Some are directly responsible for the accidental deaths of those involved in their creation; others have caused tragedy indirectly by inspiring occult movements, serial killers, copycat crimes, psychotic behavior in audiences, or bizarre and freakish coincidences. These "cursed" films include *The Exorcist, Rosemary's Baby, Twilight Zone – The Movie* and *The Crow*; films that have become notorious and compelling in their new role as inadvertent epitaphs, as documents on the subject of human mortality.

The book contains interviews with sexploitation producer David Friedman, screenwriter Antonio Passolini, director Lindsay Honey and porn actress/producer Jane Hamilton, and includes a stunning eight-page full-colour section.

CINEMA/CULTURE   Trade paperback 1 871592 85 2   256 pages   169 x 244mm   £14.95

DEATH AND DESTINY IN THE DREAM FACTORY
AN ILLUSTRATED HISTORY OF CURSED MOVIES

⑭ LOST HIGHWAYS *Jack Sargeant & Stephanie Watson*

The road movie: a complex cinematic journey that incorporates mythic themes of questing and searching, the need for being, for love, for a home and for a promise of a different future, and yet also serves as a map of current cultural desires, dreams, and fears.

Lost Highways explores the history of the road movie through a series of detailed essays on key films within the genre. Through these comprehensive and absorbing studies a clear and concise post-modern picture of the road movie emerges, tracing hitherto neglected intersections with other genres such as the western, film noir, horror, and even science fiction.

From *The Wizard Of Oz* to *Crash, Apocalypse Now* to *Vanishing Point, The Wild Bunch* to *Easy Rider*, **Lost Highways** is the definitive illustrated guide to a diverse body of film which holds at its nucleus the quintessential cinematic/cultural interchange of modern times.

Jack Sargeant is an acclaimed underground film critic, and is the author of Deathtripping and Naked Lens.

CINEMA/CULTURE   Trade paperback 1 871592 68 2   256 pages   169mm x 244mm   £14.95

AN ILLUSTRATED HISTORY OF ROAD MOVIES
Jack Sargeant & Stephanie Watson

⑮ A TASTE OF BLOOD *Christopher Wayne Curry*

The incredibly popular, violent horror films of recent decades, such as *Texas Chainsaw Massacre, Friday The 13th*, and *A Nightmare On Elm Street*, owe much of their existence to the undisputed Godfather of Gore – Herschell Gordon Lewis. In 1963 Lewis, with his monumental splatter movie Blood Feast, single-handedly changed the face of horror cinema forever.

As well as virtually inventing the gore genre, Lewis also produced a number of nudie and roughie movies, as well as sampling the full gamut of exploitation subjects ranging from wife-swapping and ESP to rock'n'roll and LSD. A Taste Of Blood details all these, plus gore classics such as *2,000 Maniacs, Gore-Gore Girls, Color Me Blood Red* and *Wizard Of Gore*, placing them in context amid the roots and development of the exploitation film.

A Taste Of Blood is a definitive study which not only chronicles Lewis' career as the master of exploitation, but also contains interviews with him and many of his former collaborators, including David F Friedman, Bill Rogers, Daniel Krogh, Mal Arnold and Hedda Lubin. These are interwoven with commentary, extremely rare photographs, ad mats, production stills, posters, and a thorough synopsis of each of Lewis' three dozen influential films. Also included is a stunning 8-page colour section of graphic screen gore.

CINEMA   Trade paperback 1 871592 91 7   256 pages   169mm x 244mm   £16.95

THE FILMS OF
HERSCHELL GORDON LEWIS

NECRONOMICON 1

Andy Black (ed)

Necronomicon Book One continues the singular, thought-provoking exploration of transgressive cinema begun by the much-respected and acclaimed magazine of the same name. The transition to annual book format has allowed for even greater depth and diversity within the journal's trademarks of progressive critique and striking photographic content.

Including: MARCO FERRERI • TEXAS CHAINSAW MASSACRE • BARBARA STEELE • FRIGHTMARE • JEAN ROLLIN • DEEP THROAT • DARIO ARGENTO LAST TANGO IN PARIS • H P LOVECRAFT • WITCHFINDER GENERAL HERSCHELL GORDON LEWIS • EVIL DEAD • ABEL FERRARA *and much more*

CINEMA   Trade Paperback   1 871592 37 2   169 x 244mm   192 pages   £12.95

NECRONOMICON 2

Andy Black (ed)

Book Two of the journal of horror and erotic cinema, continuing the thought-provoking exploration of transgressive film making begun by the first volume. With more illustrated insights into the world of celluloid sex and violence, including:

JESUS FRANCO • SADEAN CINEMA • RUSS MEYER MANSON, POLANSKI, MACBETH • NEW JAPANESE PORNO GEORGE A ROMERO • SS EXPLOITATION • BABA YAGA/CEMETERY MAN WALERIAN BOROWCZYK • DARIO ARGENTO • FEMALE VAMPIRES • SE7EN *and much more*

"Lovingly produced and amply illustrated... engaging... Heady stuff."
—Sight & Sound

CINEMA   Trade paperback   1 871592 38 2   169 x 244mm   192 pages   £12.95

MAIL ORDER FORM   *(please photocopy if you do not wish to cut up your book)*

TITLE (please tick box)	PRICE(UK)	PRICE(US)	QTY
☐ Dennis Hopper Movie Top 10	£12.95	$17.95	
☐ Harvey Keitel Movie Top 10	£12.95	$17.95	
☐ Robert De Niro Movie Top 10	£12.95	$17.95	
☐ Johnny Depp Movie Top 10	£12.95	$17.95	
☐ Killing for Culture	£14.95	$19.95	
☐ Inside Teradome	£14.95	$19.95	
☐ Deathtripping	£14.95	$19.95	
☐ Fragments of Fear	£14.95	$19.95	
☐ Desperate Visions	£14.95	$19.95	
☐ The Naked Lens	£12.95	$19.95	
☐ House of Horror	£12.95	$19.95	
☐ Meat Is Murder!	£14.95	$19.95	
☐ Eros In Hell	£14.95	$19.95	
☐ Charlie's Family	£14.95	$19.95	
☐ Renegade Sisters	£14.95	$19.95	
☐ Babylon Blue	£16.95	$22.95	
☐ Hollywood Hex	£14.95	$19.95	
☐ A Taste of Blood	£16.95	$22.95	
☐ Lost Highways	£14.95	$19.95	
☐ Necronomicon 1	£12.95	$17.95	
☐ Necronomicon 2	£12.95	$17.95	

SUBTOTAL ....

P&P ....

TOTAL ....

☐ I enclose cheque/money order/cash

☐ I wish to pay by ☐ Visa   ☐ Mastercard

Card No:

| | | | | | | | | | | | | | | | | |

Expiry Date _____

Signature _____Date _____

Name_____

Address_____

_____

_____

UK: Add 10% to total price for p&tp. EUROPE: Add 15%. Payment with order to: Creation Books, 83 Clerkenwell Road. London EC1R 5AR (£sterling only).
US: Add 10% to total price for p&tp. REST OF THE WORLD: Add 20%. Payment with order to: Creation Books, PO Box 13512, Berkeley, CA 94712 (US$ only)
or order direct from our Website at: www.creationbooks.com

CREATION BOOKS